Learning Fencing

This book was given to me by: _____

My name: _____

My birthday: _____

My address: _____

_____

Photo

I like: _____

_____

I don't like: _____

_____

What I wish for: _____

_____

LEARNING FENCING

Berndt Barth/Katrin Barth

Meyer & Meyer Sport

Original title: *Ich lerne Fechten*
© Meyer & Meyer Verlag, 2001
Translated by
AAA Translation, St. Louis, Missouri

Expert review: Anja Schache, vice-world champion foil, youth competitive sports advisor,
German Fencing Federation

British Library Cataloguing in Publication Data
A catalogue record for this book is available from the British Library

Learning Fencing
Maidenhead: Meyer & Meyer Sport (UK) Ltd., 2017
ISBN: 978-1-78255-113-3

© 2018 by Meyer & Meyer Sport, Aachen, Germany
1st reprint 2018 of the 3rd edition 2017
Auckland, Beirut, Dubai, Hägendorf, Hong Kong, Indianapolis, Cairo, Cape Town,
Manila, Maidenhead, New Delhi, Singapore, Sydney, Teheran, Vienna
Member of the World
Sports Publishers' Association (WSPA)
www.w-s-p-a.org
Printed by: Print Consult GmbH, Munich, Germany
ISBN 978-1-78255-113-3
E-mail: info@m-m-sports.com

.............Table of Contents

Caution:
The exercises and practical suggestions in this book have been carefully chosen and reviewed by the authors. However, the authors are not liable for accidents or damages of any kind incurred in connection with the content of this book.

Hi, I'm Foily,
and I will accompany you through
this book. I'm sure we'll have
lots of fun together.

In this book, you will learn lots
about fencing, and I will always be
there with you. I'm sure we'll have
lots of fun together.

In this book you will often see the following three Foily symbols:

Whenever you see this symbol, it means that Foily
has a great tip for you. He shows you mistakes and
how you can can avoid making them, or gives you
some good advice.

Here Foily shows you some exercises you can do outside of your
fencing lessons. Of course they
don't replace your lessons, but
they are a good supplement.

This is where Foily has a puzzle or a tricky question for you.
You will find the solutions and answers at the end of the
book.

You can put photos of yourself, your fencing friends, your fencing instructor, or your fencing class here.

........1 Dear Fencing Child

Was it a classmate, the well-known fencing club in your area, or watching the last fencing world championships on television? It doesn't really matter how you became interested in fencing. What matters is that you chose an amazing sport.

A fencer is:

- as fast as a sprinter.
- as dexterous as a juggler.
- as clever as a chess player.

When we first learned to fence, our fencing instructor would always tell us:

Surely you've already noticed that in a fencing club you not only fence, but you do all sorts of other sports as well. That's great, because a fencer has to be in good shape overall. For instance, running gives you endurance, jumping gives you power, gymnastics make you flexible. You can swim in summer and ski in winter. Your fencing instructor will have plenty of other good ideas for versatile training, and for making good fencers out of you.

However, you can only learn fencing by fencing!

© Foto-Zentrum Leipzig

Maybe you'll be a really successful fencer some day, but even if you won't ever be a world champion or an Olympic champion, you will find that you are getting a lot out of fencing. You learn to do a sport together with others, to give your best, and to experience victory and defeat. Plus, during P.E. or while playing outside it will be obvious to everyone that you are really athletic.

For the first few years of fencing, this book should be your regular companion. It will let you reread what you have already learned, offer tips for your lessons, give you exercises to do at home, and make suggestions for your training and for competitions. If this is your own book, feel free to make notes in it, and have fun with the puzzles.

If something in the book is different from the way your instructor explained it, just ask him or her about it. Sometimes views differ, whereby neither has to be right or wrong. After all, fencing is not a law of nature, but a sport with many different aspects that are constantly evolving. That's why rules occasionally change, and you will have to amend those in your book.

So, have a great time fencing, and enjoy the book!
The authors and Foily

How can you tell if fencing is the right sport for you, and whether or not you can become a good fencer? Answer the questions with "Yes" or "No".

	Yes	No
I love sports, and romping around.	☐	☐
I like being with other kids.	☐	☐
I am already very involved in sports.	☐	☐
I am fast and therefore probably well suited.	☐	☐
I am not afraid to fight against someone else.	☐	☐
I can assert myself.	☐	☐
I like watching fencing tournaments.	☐	☐
Fencing is something special.	☐	☐
I want to learn something special.	☐	☐
I want to be better than others, and I love to win.	☐	☐
I want to be among the best in my country.	☐	☐
I want to be really famous some day.	☐	☐

If you answered most of the questions with "Yes", then you've picked the right sport.

.... 2 About the Fight to the Death

What do D'Artagnan, Zorro, and the Man with the Iron Mask have in common?

They could fence, – and how!

Well, they had to, because it was the only the way these heroes could prevail and more importantly, stay alive. Their weapon was primarily the epee.

You've probably heard of duels. They were all about honor, women, or power. But fortunately we are past the times when differences of opinion were settled with deadly weapons. Those times should never come back. Differences of opinion must be settled peacefully.

With Club, Dagger, and Sword

Even long ago opponents searched for aids in the "one on one" fight. Those fights were settled with clubs, sticks, swords, or daggers.

It was a good way to fend off the attacker and strike him at the same time. Often such a fight would end with the death of one of the opponents.

From Deadly Duels to Fencing as a Sport

The development of fencing as a sport with "precision touch" began in the 15th century. Gunpowder had already been invented, and fire arms were used for serious fights. The heavy suit of armor had become too weighty and cumbersome. Lighter weapons were needed, which the fencer could handle more swiftly. Duels were still fought. Anyone worth his salt and with a love for life trained with well-known fencing instructors. Later on less dangerous weapons were used for practice, and from those the sporting weapons of today evolved. Rules were established for epee, saber, and foil fencing, and tournaments were held.

In the beginning, fencing was mostly a men's sport. Fortunately this has changed. Today girls and women fence with foil, epee, and saber, just like men and boys do, and when we talk about fencing in the book, we naturally refer to girls as well as boys.

Since the first Olympic Games of modern times (1896) fencing has been a part of the Olympic program. That is why fencing is also referred to as a "classical sport". Today there are more than a million fencers in over 100 countries around the world, who train at nearly 50,000 fencing clubs.

You chose a great sport!

Hitting Your Mark Without Being Hit Yourself

The most important part of fencing is touching your opponent without being touched yourself. This rule is also applied in dueling, the difference being that in a duel any touch could be deadly.

As you already know, in today's fencing the objective is no longer to score a fatal hit. On the contrary, every precaution is taken to protect the fencer. The protective gear is designed to prevent injuries. That is also why the instructors and referees are so strict when it comes to safety. Fencing without protection, proper clothing, or with a defective mask is not permitted, in spite of the safe sporting weapons.

If you are well prepared and follow the directions of the fencing instructor, you won't have to be afraid, because fencing will not be dangerous.
You can really go on the attack without being worried about hurting your friend. After all, you want to touch and defeat your opponent.

That's what's so great about fencing. You can really fight without getting hurt or injured. Well, occasionally you may get a bruise on your arm or leg, but it's no big deal.

What's awesome too is that anyone can learn to fence!

Big or small

Skinny or not so skinny

Big biceps or not so big

Boy or girl

Healthy or with a disability

Pictogramm

Perhaps you have seen different sports depicted as drawings or symbols on television, in the newspaper, on stickers or posters. These symbols are called pictograms. The drawing is very simple, yet everyone immediately recognizes the sport it represents. Artists constantly create new symbols for big competitions and events.

This is a pictogram for fencing.

How would you illustrate hockey using very simple lines? Here is a place for your ideas!

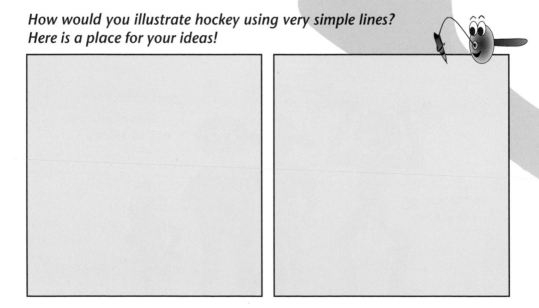

Fencing in Germany

In Germany the association uniting all fencers is called:

DFB
(German Fencing
Federation)

*The logo of your
fencing association*

*Write down the name of
the national association
for fencers in your
country and your club:*

_____

_____

*The logo of your
club*

_____

_____

*If you would like to learn more about the history or get
some current information, check out the Internet.*

········· 3 Hi there, Peter!

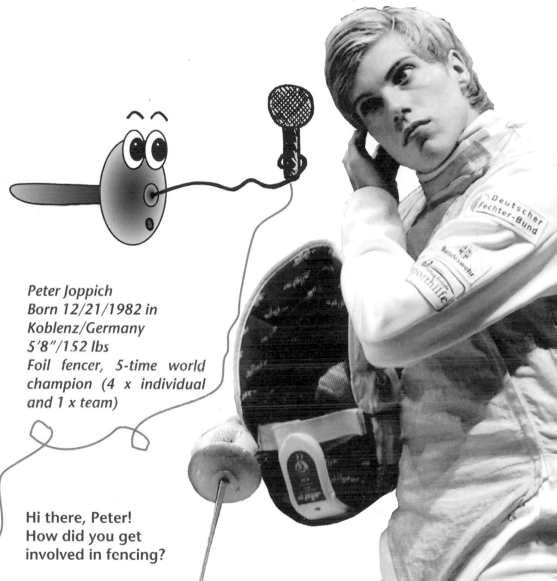

Peter Joppich
Born 12/21/1982 in
Koblenz/Germany
5'8"/152 lbs
Foil fencer, 5-time world
champion (4 x individual
and 1 x team)

Hi there, Peter!
How did you get
involved in fencing?

As a child I was fascinated by knights and musketeers. Even back then I followed sports on television and when I was 5 1/2 years old, I watched the 1988 Seoul Olympics. I was so excited about the success of the German fencers that I told my parents: "I want to become a knight like Anja on television!" Of course I was referring to Anja Fichtel, who had just won Olympic gold.

19

What do you love about fencing?

I love that it is an attractive and exciting sport, man against man, the dynamics and speed of movement, as well as the fencers' extreme power of concentration. These are all attributes that make this sport so interesting.

What does it take to be a good fencer?

Of course it takes talent and very diligent training. Add to that reaction speed, the ability to concentrate, and mental toughness (even when it is difficult to handle defeat)!). And a fencer must enjoy the exercise and the contest of a duel.

You are extremely successful. What are your strengths?

I would say my speed, mental toughness, and my absolute desire to win.

You have accomplished so much already – three individual world championships and team gold, silver, and bronze. Do you have goals for the future?

Of course I still have goals! I would like to win an Olympic medal and I want to continue to win more medals in the coming years.

Do you have time for other hobbies in addition to your training? What do you do in your free time?

When I have time I like to play soccer and watch soccer games and Formula 1 racing. I like to ski in winter. I enjoy going to the movies, listening to music, or going shopping with my girlfriend Ina.

Do you have any tips for the young up-and-coming fencers?

Believe in yourself!
Never give up in a duel!
Practice diligently!

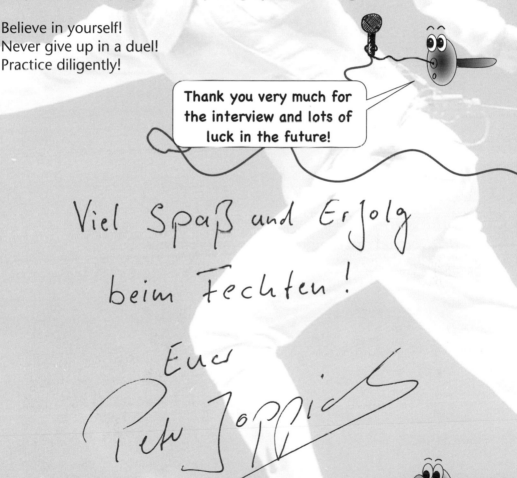

Thank you very much for the interview and lots of luck in the future!

Viel Spaß und Erfolg beim Fechten!

Euer
Peter Joppich

If you would like to know more about Peter Joppich, check out the Internet.

Which fencer would you like to interview?

_____

What would you ask him or her?

_____

_____

_____

_____

_____

Here you can collect autographs or paste pictures.

.... 4 No Pain, no Gain

Surely you have day-dreamed about being the best, and everyone else cheering and admiring you in amazement.

With a medal around your neck and a certificate in your hand you accept congratulations from your buddies, your instructor, and your parents.

But wait, just dreaming about it doesn't get you there! Being a success requires much diligence and lots and lots of practice. If you want to be a good fencer, and maybe even be better than the others, you have to practice often and diligently. That's not always easy, and it may not always be loads of fun.

If you want to be a good fencer, maybe even better than the others, you have to practice often and diligently. That's not always easy and isn't always fun right away.

Diligence leads to success!

23

Goals

When you begin with fencing, you will need to answer the following questions:

> What is my goal?

> What do I need to reach my goal?

> How can I reach my goal?

1. What is my goal? Why am I working so hard?

You have to know what you want. If you don't have a goal, practicing soon won't be any fun.

A fencer's most important goal is to win against another fencer. First you try to win against other fencers from your practice group. If you lose you just keep practicing until you can defeat them. Once you have achieved that, you'll want to win against stronger and better fencers. So you keep setting yourself higher goals. That's what our best fencers did, until they became club champion, regional champion, national champion, or even world and Olympic champion.

Why do you want to learn fencing? Write down your goals here!

_____

_____

_____

2. What do I need to reach my goal?

You ask how you can improve your performance.

And the answer is: All of the fencing exercises are necessary to improve your performance. This includes gymnastics, leg work, partner exercises, exercises with a target and in front of the mirror, as well as lessons with the fencing instructor. You may think that some of these exercises aren't much fun, that they are boring and much too strenuous. But you have to keep in mind that all of these exercises are tools for reaching your goal. If you know that good leg work is very important for a fencer, and that you can only improve this with lots of practice, then you will have more fun practicing. Then you will quickly see improvement, and you will see that with lots of repetition you will get better and better.

3. How can I reach my goal?

How can you improve your performance bypracticing?

As long as the exercises are easy and lax, your muscles are doing only the minimum. Only when they become strenuous and it hurts just a little and moving isn't as easy, are your muscles being strengthened. So you have to exert and strain yourself to make progress. If you ever don't fence for a while, you will notice that you have digressed a little and have to catch up again.

The more diligently and frequently ou practice, the better you will be!

Physical Fitness is important

> Oh boy! I can't go on! I'm totally wiped out!

Oh dear! What's wrong with Foily? After fencing for half an hour he is so exhausted that he can barely stand up.

Has that ever happened to you? Do you also get winded easily and lose your strength quickly? Then you need to work on your fitness level!

What should a good fencer be able to do? Cross out the things that are not as important. If we forgot anything, write it down!

Run fast		Play the flute
Control the ball well	Ski	
		Have good mobility
Jump well	React at lightning speed	
		Fight courageously
Good concentration	Play sports for an hour	Tell jokes well

What is physical fitness?

When you fence you always have to be alert, move quickly, nimbly wield the blade, and launch powerful attacks. Tournaments can be long, you are called to compete again and again, and each time you must engage the opponent with total concentration. Are you able to do this long-term? Then you're in good shape.

If not, fencing soon won't be fun anymore and you should work on your fitness level. You can do that primarily by practicing regularly.

What do you need?

Good fencers have body tension, move quickly, can lunge at lightening speed, and perform powerful parries. To do so they need **strong** hands, arms and legs, back and abdominal muscles.

The lunge is deep and the blade must be guided skilfully. Excellent **mobility** is important here.

Furthermore it is important that fencers are able to move at lightening speed and react in an instant. This requires **speed**.

You need good **endurance** to sustain physical exertion for an extended period of time. Then you won't get winded as easily during quick movements, focused bouts and long tournaments. And when it does get strenuous you recover quickly and feel fit again.

During training you will not only practice footwork and fencing with partners. Your coach will most certainly do lots of gymnastics, strength exercises, running games, and much more. Make sure you participate well because all of this improves your fitness level!

THIS IS HOW YOU CAN PRACTICE

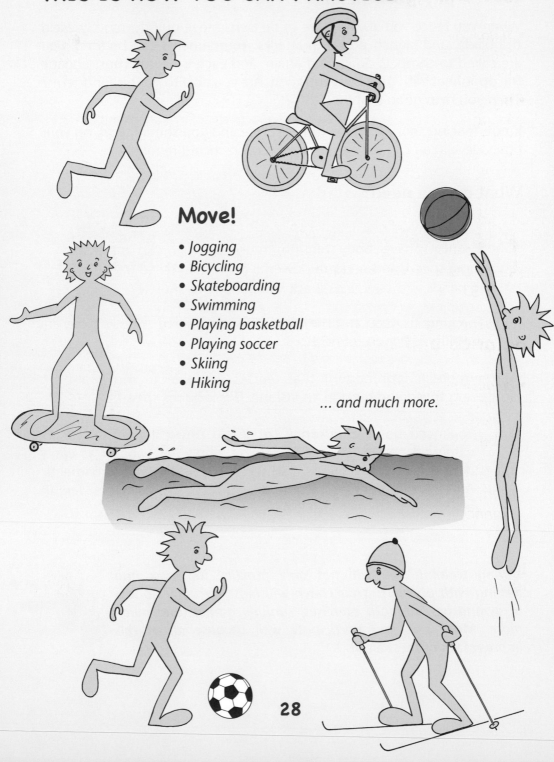

Move!

- *Jogging*
- *Bicycling*
- *Skateboarding*
- *Swimming*
- *Playing basketball*
- *Playing soccer*
- *Skiing*
- *Hiking*

... and much more.

28

Fast and agile

- *Slalom run*
  Set up a slalom course using poles, cones or other objects.
  Who can get the fastest time without making a mistake?

- *High and low*
  Set up a course with several low hurdles in a row. The runner jumps over
  the first hurdle, crawls under the next hurdle, jumps over the next one, etc.
  Who gets the best time?

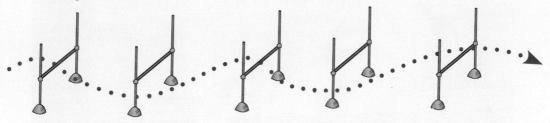

Balance and dexterity

- *Balancing*
  Balance on a chalk line or a beam. You may find low
  walls in your neighborhood or fallen trees in the forest to
  balance on.

- *Dexterity exercises*
  Many athletic exercises require dexterity and skill. Try inline
  skating, ice skating, walking on stilts, riding a mountain bike or bicycle.
  Have you ever juggled?

Which sport do you like to play besides hockey?
Write it down here.

_____

_____

.... 5 The Equipment

Just like athletes from other sports, fencers are proud of their particular attire.

But the special fencing attire is not just about looking good. It provides the wearer with important protection. In the sport of fencing, safety is number one. That's why there are special regulations for the protective clothing and equipment.

But, no worries! You don't have to have to have the complete outfit when you sign up for fencing. Gym clothes and tennis shoes are generally good enough for the beginning exercises, which are performed without a partner.

Your fencing instructor will let you borrow a fencing glove and a weapon for your first lessons. You will most likely also get to use a mask and a fencing jacket.

If you are having fun fencing and you definitely want to continue, it would be best if you bought your own fencing equipment!

© Foto-Zentrum Leipzig

The Fencing Attire

Fencers wear a **fencing suit** (Whites) made out of white Kevlar, a very tough fabric. The fencing suit consists of a fencing jacket and knee breeches. To complete the outfit you will need an **underjacket** (must pass 800 N puncture test), **stockings**, non-skid **fencing shoes**, and a **fencing glove** for the hand wielding the weapon. The female fencers wear a **chest protector** under their fencing suit. The face is protected by a **wire mask**.

Of course a fencer must have at least one weapon as part of his or her practice equipment: a foil, an epee, or a saber. Fencers under twelve years of age (student class) use special smaller weapons.

For fencing with an electronic scoring aid you also need a **body cable** and an "**electronic weapon**", which indicates the hits on the electronic scoring apparatus. In foil fencing and saber fencing, an electroconductive vest or Lamé (a brocade vest) covers the valid target area. In saber fencing the mask and the glove must also be covered with electroconductive material.

All this stuff gets packed into a fencing bag that is long enough to accommodate the weapons.

Always make sure that all pieces of equipment meet national and international regulations.

Fencing is certainly not the cheapest sport, but it is something special. You can probably find out from your instructor or through your club where you can buy the right fencing equipment in your area. Chances are you can even buy used pieces of equipment from older athletes.

Fencing Equipment as Part of a Wish List

You know how your parents and grandparents always ask you about your Christmas or birthday wishes?

Why not suggest they help pay for a new fencing outfit?

Everything packed?

Oh boy!
This jacket is
way too big!

Imagine you forget to bring a piece of your equipment, like for instance your fencing jacket, to your lesson or to a tournament.

If you are lucky you can borrow one. Of course it won't fit properly and will either be too loose or too tight.
That could be embarrassing!

Your parents could of course help pack your bag, but every player is responsible for his own complete and clean equipment!

The Checklist

Use a Checklist for every lesson and for every tournament, so this won't happen to you. Everything you have packed is checked off with a pencil. The next time you pack your bag, the old checks are erased and new ones put in their place. On the blank lines write down the things that are important to you, but you tend to forget about, like drinks, shampoo, or a hat in winter.

Checklist

Weapons ☐

Mask ☐

Plastron ☐

Fencing jacket ☐

Fencing breeches ☐

Stockings ☐

Shoes ☐

Glove ☐

Cable ☐

Fencing pass ☐

_____ ☐

_____ ☐

_____ ☐

_____ ☐

You should be able to use this checklist for your next fencing lesson or tournament.

Some important safety rules

- Check your fencing clothes and equipment at home when you are packing your bag. The fencing suit should not have any holes in it, no missing buttons or Velcro closures, and the zipper has to work. Check the wire screen on your mask too.

- Always wear your complete fencing outfit when fencing with a partner. That also includes having your stockings pulled all the way up.

- When fencing with a partner, both fencers must wear their mask. Even if you just want to briefly demonstrate something – always wear your mask!

- Check your weapon for possible fractures, and make sure the tips of the practice weapons are protected. This is part of fencing fairness. Your partner is supposed to take some hits during practice, and being struck with an unprotected weapon can hurt and cause injury.

- Never run your unprotected hand along the blade of your weapon. The tiny chinks in the metal can hurt you.

- Make sure that your partner is well-protected as well. Tell him or her if you notice a defect on their equipment, and don't start to fence until the problem has been fixed.

- Pay close attention to the instructions of your fencing instructor. Never wave your weapon about uncontrollably. You could easily hurt one of your buddies unintentionally.

- Outside of the gym your weapon should always stay in your fencing bag. You can show the weapon to your friends, but do not allow them to perform any fencing moves. If they want to try it, take them with you to the gym. They can probably borrow the necessary protective clothing there. Then they will very quickly see that fencing isn't that easy, and they will have a little more respect for you and your sport.

37

M	H	K	A	T	R	M	G	S	G	V	O	U	I	L
H	F	O	P	A	I	T	T	B	K	O	L	S	F	X
I	E	C	H	P	R	O	W	O	K	S	A	B	E	R
A	N	G	X	U	C	L	I	D	C	A	F	E	N	I
S	C	L	M	K	M	D	A	Y	C	L	O	N	C	A
R	I	P	I	H	P	Z	E	C	T	O	I	T	I	K
L	N	M	A	S	K	T	A	S	K	L	L	N	O
E	G	C	E	S	P	I	S	B	M	U	D	U	G	L
S	J	L	E	U	J	A	N	L	A	V	L	O	S	T
S	A	U	A	W	E	B	P	E	V	B	O	W	H	Y
R	C	A	R	G	Z	P	K	N	A	F	R	O	O	R
P	K	N	B	D	D	Z	E	P	U	M	J	Y	E	K
L	E	O	K	G	L	O	V	E	C	P	Z	U	S	A
U	T	N	A	E	G	A	S	L	V	E	F	E	L	M
K	L	O	G	W	E	G	B	S	L	N	A	H	U	U
C	E	F	R	D	P	T	M	B	D	A	I	R	R	I

1

Find nine pieces of fencing equipment – horizontally, vertically, or diagonally

2

Find the differences between drawing 1 and drawing 2. There are total nine!

1

2

38

...............6 No Weapons, no Fencing

The most important thing in fencing is, of course, the weapon. In fencing, the weapons are the sports equipment, just like a ball is the sports equipment in ball sports.

Three Different Weapons Used in the Sport of Fencing:

Here you can see how the different parts of the weapons are called. You will also notice that the saber is a little shorter than the other weapons.

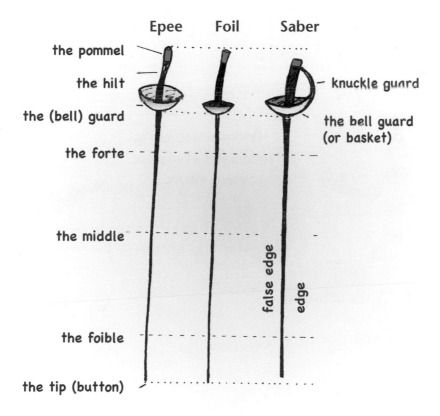

| | Epee | Foil | Saber |

the pommel

the hilt — knuckle guard

the (bell) guard — the bell guard (or basket)

the forte

the middle

false edge · edge

the foible

the tip (button)

On the foil and the epee, all the names of the parts of the weapons are the same. On the saber, the bell guard is sometimes also called the **basket**, and the piece connecting the **guard** and the **pommel** is called the **knuckle guard**. The **bell** separates the handle from the blade and serves to protect the hand. If you take a closer look at a **blade** you will notice that it gets thinner as it tapers off.

But be careful when you touch the blade!

As you already know, kids under twelve years of age fence with special smaller weapons. They are not strong enough yet to practice and fence easily and quickly with the large weapons.

The Grips

It is very important to hold the weapon tightly at the grip. This will allow you to handle the weapon swiftly, and your partner won't be able to knock it out of your hand easily.

Surely you have noticed that the different weapons have different handles.

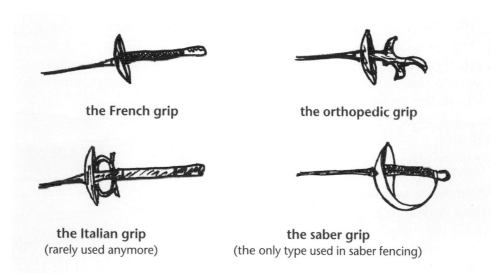

the French grip   the orthopedic grip

the Italian grip   the saber grip
(rarely used anymore)   (the only type used in saber fencing)

Many foil and epee fencers use the orthopedic grip. However, for the basic training it would advisable to practise with a French grip. This helps to develop finger strength and dexterity.

Holding the Grip

The way you hold the different grips is similar, but not exactly the same!

The hand position on the **orthopedic grip** (sometimes also called "pistol grip") is very simple, since the position of the fingers is predetermined by the particular shape. The weapon is guided with your thumb and index finger.

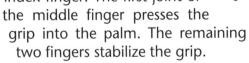

On the **French grip** you place the area between the first and second joint of your index finger on the underside of the handle. The distance to the inside of the bell guard is slightly less than 1/4 inch. The thumb holds the grip from the top, opposite the index finger. The weapon is held and guided by the pressure of thumb against index finger. The first joint of the middle finger presses the grip into the palm. The remaining two fingers stabilize the grip.

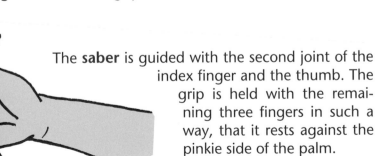

The **saber** is guided with the second joint of the index finger and the thumb. The grip is held with the remaining three fingers in such a way, that it rests against the pinkie side of the palm.

Nimble Fingers – Quick Blade

Do you remember how hard it was to write your first letters, or how difficult it was to use a knife and fork?

Now you would say: "No problem! It's automatic." Well, sure, you've practiced long enough. But try to eat with chopsticks like the Chinese do. You'd probably have to practice that first, too.
It's all in the proper handling!

It is the same with a fencing weapon. It is the fencer's most important tool.

Ways You Can Practice

1 *The exercises begin with some finger gymnastics.*

Place your finger tips together and practice this: Press hard and then relax your fingers again.

Five or six times are enough. Always do this before you pick up a weapon, at the fencing hall, too.

2 **It is important to be able to move thumb and index finger independently from the other fingers.**

Press the tips of your thumb and index finger together and practice the following with the remaining fingers:

bend   *and*   *extend*

3 **For this next exercise you will need a stick, or a wooden spoon, or something similar.**

You pick up the stick with thumb and index finger and hold it with the other fingers. Now you can practice:

alternate holding   *and*   *letting go.*

4 *An exercise specifically for saber fencers.*

Again you will need a stick, but this time hold it like a saber.

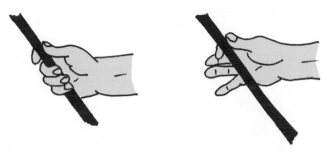

Now practice: *Hold*   *and*   *let go.*

5 *Strong hands*

In order to hold on to the weapon securely you need strong hands and nimble fingers. This exercise will strengthen your hands.

Find a stick and tie a piece of string to it. Tie a rock or some other heavy object to the other end of the string. Now start winding the string around the stick, and then unwind it again. Continue to alternate between the two. Your fingers should move quickly. Stop if it starts to hurt. Loosen up your hands and then try again.

You can do this exercise several times each day.

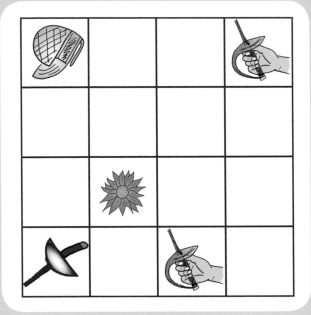

1 Each symbol appears in every row, column, and diagonal.

Draw the remaining symbols in the appropriate squares!

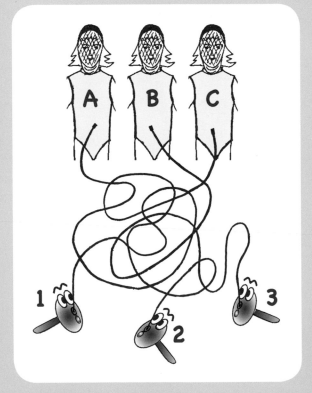

2 Which fencer was hit by which foil fencer?

First try to match them with only your eyes (without tracing them with your finger or a pencil)!

....................7 The Three Disciplines of Fencing

As we mentioned before, there are certain stipulations in the sport of fencing which are defined by regulations.

These are called conventions.

The most important ones are:

The weapons:	epee, foil, and saber
Type of touch:	thrust or cut
The target area:	where is a touch valid?
The priority:	when is a touch valid?

The Three Types of Weapons

You already know the three different types of weapons. No matter if you're a girl or a boy, you can fence with any of these weapons. That wasn't always the case. For a long time women could only fence with the foil, then the epee was added. Now women and girls also fence with the saber.

The type of weapon used for the basic training differs. It isn't really relevant since you can learn the basics on any one of them. Later you can decide if you want to fence with the foil, the epee, or the saber.

You can learn the basics of fencing with each of the three weapons.

Foil Fencing

The foil is the lightest of the three weapons. The blade has a tetragonal shape. The bell guard is also smaller than on the other weapons.

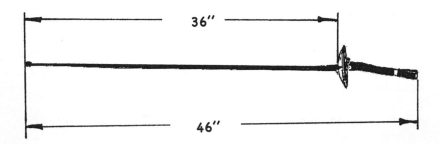

 **The valid target area is the trunk (filled in black in the illustration).**

Touches on hands, arms, legs, and on the head are invalid. As you can see in the illustrations, there is a small difference between the front and the back.

In foil fencing priority rules when both fencers touch at the same time. The fencer who attacks first, or the fencer who successfully repels an attack and then launches an attack him- or herself, scores on the touch.

This is explained in detail in Chapter 10, "Keeping things straight".

The foil is a thrusting weapon. This means that only touches made with the tip of the blade (button) are valid.

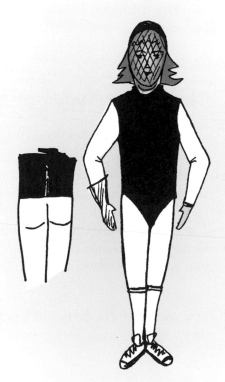

Epee Fencing

The epee has a trihedronic (triple edge) blade and a large bell guard.

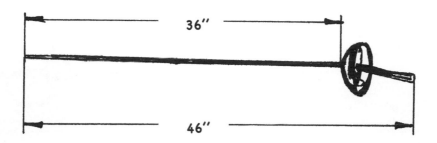

36"

46"

 The complete fencer from head to toe is considered a valid target area (black). That means that touches to the feet are also valid.

Priority does not apply in epee fencing. Whoever gets the first touch is right and scores. If both fencers touch at the same time both have been touched, and both score.

Like the foil, the epee is a thrusting weapon.

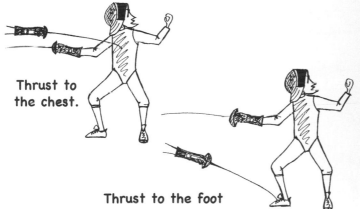

Thrust to the chest.

Thrust to the foot

Saber Fencing

The saber is a slightly different weapon. It is lighter than the epee and the foil, and the cross-section of the blade is almost rectangular. The bell guard, also called a basket, has a totally different shape.

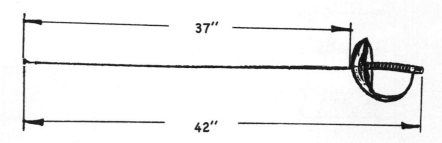

37"

42"

 **In saber fencing, the target area is the whole trunk, including the head and arms (black).**

In saber fencing, as in foil fencing, priority rules.

The saber is a cutting and thrusting weapon. That means you can score with a thrust of the tip as well as a cut of the blade. It is irrelevant whether the cut touches with the edge, the headfalse edge, or the flat side.

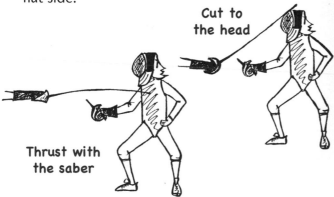

Cut to
the head

Thrust with
the saber

That is also why in saber fencing the weapon is held a little differently, as we already mentioned when we talked about how to hold the grips. The fencing stance in saber fencing is also somewhat different from foil fencing.

Color in the shapes according to the legend!

1 green	4 brown	7 black
2 dark blue	5 yellow	8 pink
3 light blue	6 red	9 grey

........8 What You Need to Know About Technique

If you want to read a good book you need to know your ABCs, and to be able to swim you need to know the correct arm and leg movements.

A fencer needs to learn the proper technique before he or she can fence!

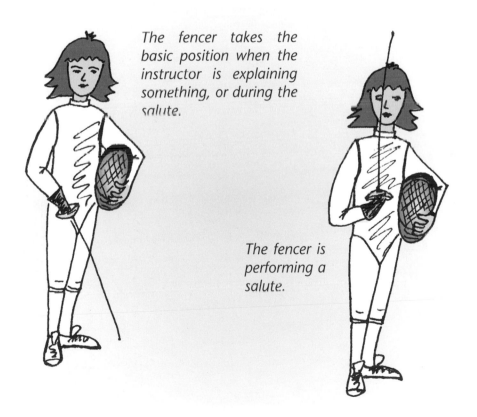

The fencer takes the basic position when the instructor is explaining something, or during the salute.

The fencer is performing a salute.

The "Salute" Greeting

Before and after a bout, the fencers greet the opponent, the referee, and if present, the audience.

This is not just being friendly and polite,
but it is also in the rule book.

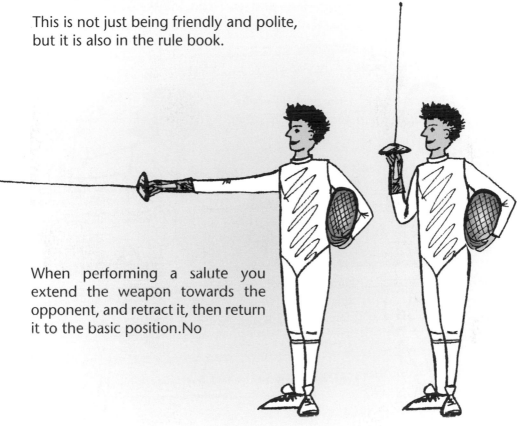

When performing a salute you extend the weapon towards the opponent, and retract it, then return it to the basic position.No

A great way to practice the correct fencing stance and the salute to the opponent is in front of a large mirror.

The Fencing Stance

The fencing stance is the most convenient stance for the fencer, because:

- The leg muscles are engaged, and you can immediately launch an attack without the opponent being able to read your intentions.

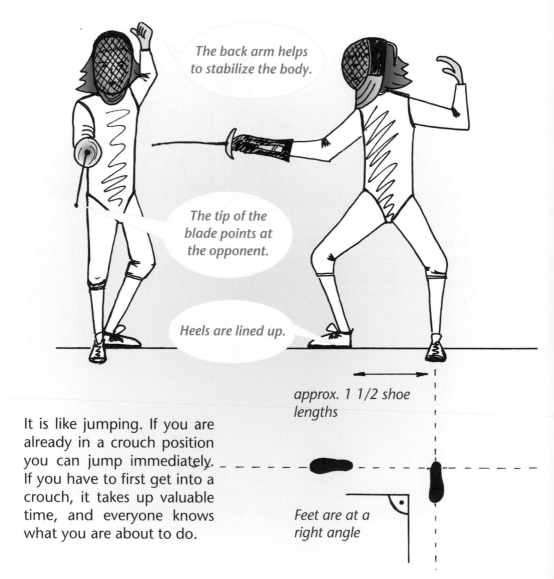

The back arm helps to stabilize the body.

The tip of the blade points at the opponent.

Heels are lined up.

approx. 1 1/2 shoe lengths

Feet are at a right angle

It is like jumping. If you are already in a crouch position you can jump immediately. If you have to first get into a crouch, it takes up valuable time, and everyone knows what you are about to do.

- From this position you can do the forward and backward steps as well as the lunge.

- The arm bearing the weapon is the most forward, and you are showing the opponent the smallest target area.

- Having your feet at a right angle helps you keep your balance and gives you a solid base.

No matter if the hand bearing the weapon is the right or the left:

The head is straight and tilted slightly forward.

The shoulder girdle is relaxed.

Hip, knee, and ankle of the front leg form a straight line.

The lunging leg is always the front leg.

The supporting leg is always the back leg.

The line is the imaginary line that intersects your heels when your feet are at a right angle in the fencing stance.

Point In Line

means that you are in fencing stance
and have both arms extended.

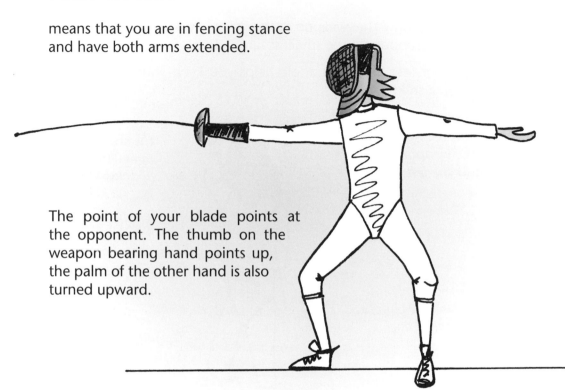

The point of your blade points at
the opponent. The thumb on the
weapon bearing hand points up,
the palm of the other hand is also
turned upward.

Do you know how a cat catches a mouse?

It watches the mouse.
it sneaks up close,
then retreats
if it thinks it might be discovered.

It waits until
it has found the right
distance to the mouse.
Then it can catch its victim with a single leap.

The fencer behaves similarly!

Advance and Retreat

In single combat the attacker is trying to get as close as possible to the opponent!

In a wrestling match the two wrestlers stand close enough to each other that the opponent can be gripped. Boxers prefer a distance from which they can strike the opponent with an extended arm, and still are able to dodge a counterattack with a small backward move.

Fencers keep a wider distance from each other. The arm is "lengthened" by the weapon in hand, and the distance is thereby increased. The distance between two fencers is called the measure.

Fencing Movements

You have to move quickly, almost cat-like, if you want to get close to your opponent or want to evade an advance. For this purpose there is a particular step technique which the fencer has to practice a lot. In order to perform the steps correctly you have to always check to see if you are in a proper fencing stance.

- The feet are at a right angle. Also, the front foot points to the opponent, the back foot points to the side at a right angle.

- There is a distance of approx. 1 1/2 shoe lengths between the feet.

- The knees are bent as if you wanted to sit between them.

- The torso is erect, the shoulders relaxed, and the head points to the opponent.

- The free arm is "rolled up" (bent) behind you, and the weapon bearing arm is also bent, but not "stuck" against the body.

The Forward Step

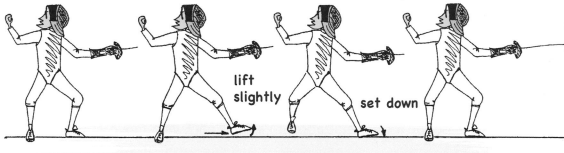

lift slightly   set down

fencing stance   push off quickly   set your feet in pursuit   fencing stance

With one forward step you get approximately one shoe length closer to your opponent. The front foot leads while the back foot follows.

Try to avoid making these typical mistakes!

This fencer is leaning too far back and is lifting his front leg up too high. It looks as if he is going to climb up on a chair. The "climber's" weapon is pointing up into the air and not at the opponent. Just lift your toes a little and your heel will glide across the floor.

This fencer is standing as upright as a soldier and there isn't enough space between the feet. This isn't a good fencing stance. As a "soldier" you would not be able to move quickly enough.

The Backward Step

A backward step is taken to evade the opponent or to change the measure. Think of the sequence as being exactly opposite to the step forward. First the back foot is set back by approximately one foot length. The front foot follows by gliding back.

Try to avoid making these typical mistakes!

This fencer is also standing up too straight and he is letting his back arm hang down. He looks like he is taking a break. This is not a fencing stance.

This fencer is lifting his back leg up too high. (Like a dog at a tree...)

- Technique worth knowing Set your feet, don't "shuffle". The torso remains erect and still. Only the legs move.

- The opponent must not be able to anticipate your intended move.

Some fencers use a leap, a double quick, or a cross-step for their forward- and backward moves. These steps are not used much anymore, but may be your fencing instructor will show you the technique.

When you go for a walk or a run you don't have to pay attention to your feet anymore, because you've been walking and running since you were really small!

When you are fencing your movements need to happen the same way, without your paying attention to your feet and your steps. Everything is so totally automatic that you can fully concentrate on your opponent and the planned attack.

You can easily practice getting a feel for the sequence of moves at home (preferably in front of a mirror).

Attention, mistakes!

Imagine your training partner in the same stances as the five stick figures below. Which mistakes do you recognize, and how would you correct them?

You will find the answers on the solution page!

Some exercises

1 *Assume a fencing stance and practice the following step sequences:*

- *One step forward, one step back.*
- *Two steps forward, one step back.*
- *One step forward, two steps back, on step forward.*
- Two small quick steps forward, one big step back.
- Two quick steps back, three big steps forward, one step back.

Try to think of some step sequences you can practice, and write them down. Don't look at your feet and close your eyes. You can also practice this together with your friends. Check and help each other. A training partner sometimes sees mistakes more easily than you do.

_____

_____

_____

2 *Steps on a line*

Take a large piece of paper (wallpaper would be good) and draw a line on it. That is your "line".

Stand on the line and practice your step sequences without looking down. Check to see if you are still on the line after the last step in each sequence.

Check your fencing stance.

3 *Fencing grid*

You can also use a grid (see illustration).

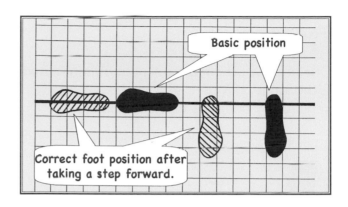

Assume a fencing stance on the grid and trace around your feet with a marker. Check where you are after taking one step forward, and by how many boxes you are off. After taking one step forward and one step back you should be standing in the traced "feet", as well as if you take two steps forward and two steps back.

As you already know now, only the fencer who has a good fencing stance can move quickly and easily in a bout!

The Lunge

One of the most important and most often used leg movements in fencing is the lunge. It is used in almost every attack. By doing a lunge you can very quickly get close to the opponent.

1 "On Guard" is the stance you are in when you are in a standing position, or after a forward or backward step.

2 First the weapon bearing arm is extended. The weight is taken slightly off the front leg (also called the lunging leg) and lifted just a little, as if taking a forward step. The free arm begins to "roll up".

3 The lower leg is "thrust" forward forcefully; the back leg is quickly extended.

This leg remains stationary during the whole lunge until the very end, and it is called the "pivot leg".

Practice doing a few lunges every morning and every evening (don't forget to warm up).

You'll notice that you will get faster and faster. Always check your form. A mirror or your parents can help you with that.

4 The opponent is touched when you reach your highest speed. You land heel first.

5 Lastly the active force of the lunge is checked.

Make sure that your torso remains erect while performing the lunge.

Attention, mistakes!

The lunge must be performed correctly in order to be quick and successful. Can you recognize the mistakes these figures are making?

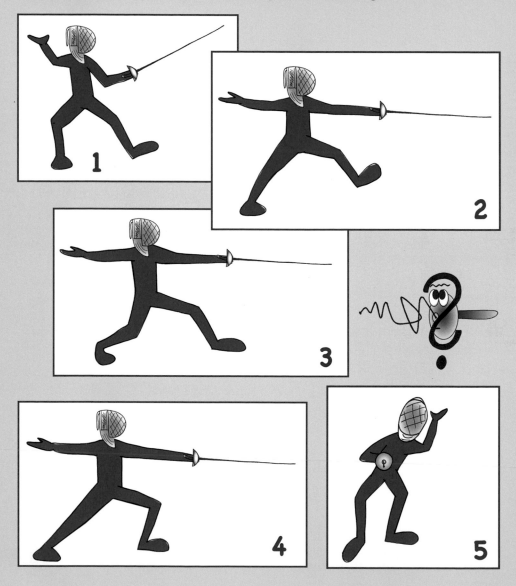

Recovery From the Lunge

If you performed the lunge correctly you should be able to recover from it quickly.

This is important because if your attack was unsuccessful you have to be careful that your opponent doesn't touch you instead.

Ok, so let's get back to the fencing stance.

This is how it works:

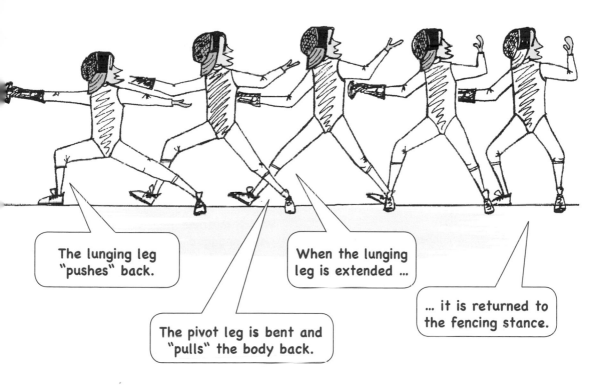

The lunging leg "pushes" back.

When the lunging leg is extended ...

... it is returned to the fencing stance.

The pivot leg is bent and "pulls" the body back.

When stepping backward the pivot leg is bent and "pulls" the body back.

Attention, mistakes!

Can you recognize the mistakes these figures are making?

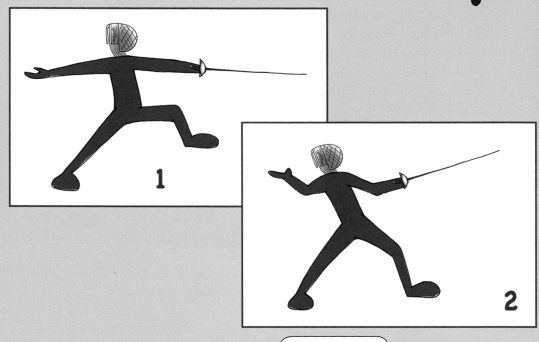

How you can practice

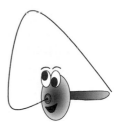

You need to practice lunges again and again. That is very, very important!

In the beginning it is often difficult and your legs may ache. Even world champions practice lunges during every training session so they can perform them more quickly and more sudden.

Now you can incorporate the lunge into your forward and backward step drills.

- *One forward step, lunge.*

- *One forward step, one backward step, lunge.*

- *Lunge, two backward steps, one forward step, lunge.*

Write down your own step-lunge combinations to practice:

_____   _____

_____

_____

_____

When you practice these drills at home, make sure you do some warm-up exercises before you begin. This warms up the muscles and stretches them. If you don't warm up first you could injure yourself!

Have fun practicing! If you want to, show your parents what you have learned so far.

In a fencing bout the objective is to score as many valid touches on the opponent as possible. As you already know, in foil and epee fencing you may only use the thrust, and in saber fencing only the thrust (also called a stab) and the cut.

Setting Up the Thrust

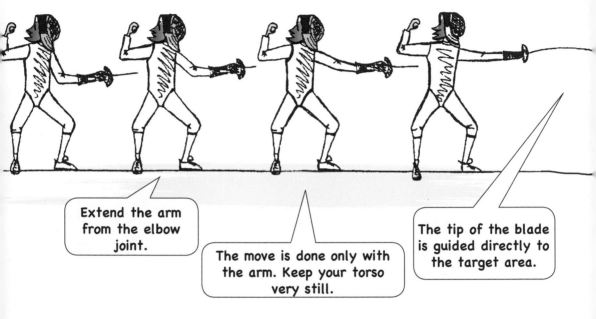

Extend the arm from the elbow joint.

The move is done only with the arm. Keep your torso very still.

The tip of the blade is guided directly to the target area.

Now get in front of a mirror again, and stand on the line you drew, or just somewhere in your room.

- *Practice the direct thrust as you see it in the illustration.*
- *Practice the direct thrust with your eyes closed, then open your eyes and check your form.*

- *Forward step, thrust.*
- *Backward step, forward step, thrust.*
- *Forward step, thrust, two quick backward steps.*

Think of some combinations of your own to practice, and write them down.

72

Attention, mistakes!

Can you recognize the mistakes these figures are making?

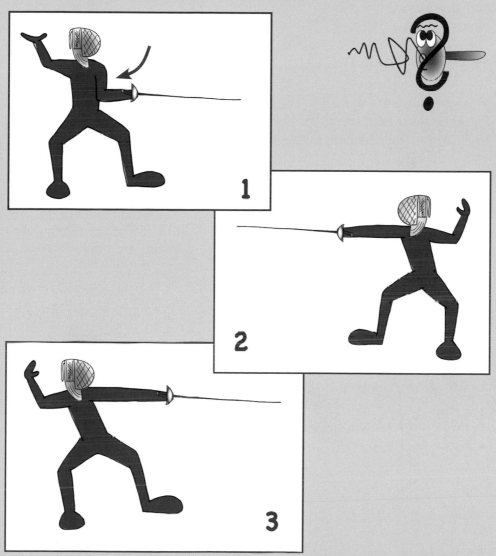

When you practice, pay attention to proper form. The illustrations of mistakes will help you to correct yourself.

Cuts and Stabs with a Saber

You cut with the saber and the thrust is called a stab. We have already explained how the saber is held and handled. Because this weapon is handled a little differently, the move on target is also slightly different.

The Cut

Important cuts are the cut to the head, the cut to the flank, and the cut to the chest. However, the cut to the flank and the cut to the chest are difficult to illustrate. Your fencing instructor can demonstrate these much better.

The cut to the head

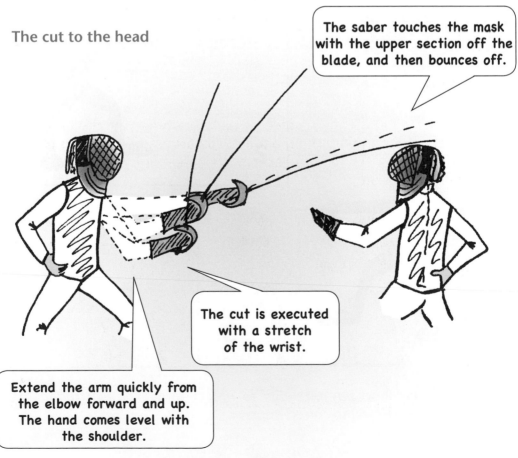

There are two major mistakes you need to avoid making:

The cut should not start with a drawing back of the arm. It takes too much time, and your opponent can quickly see what you are about to do.

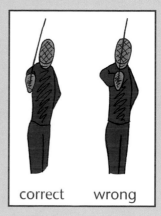

When you extend the arm, don't move your hand to the inside. Your opponent could touch you on the outside of your arm. That area would no longer be protected.

correct   wrong

The Stab

When performing a stab, the saber is turned, so that your thumb points to the left during the forward motion (if you are left-handed your thumb points to the right). You can easily check this. Upon impact the saber should bend upward.

As you can see the movements are just like the ones in foil and epee fencing.

Positions and Position Changes

Before we get to the positions let's talk about the importance of the opening. The opening is the part of the body that can be targeted.

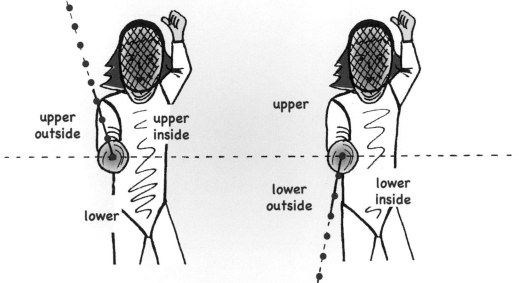

Imagine a horizontal line that runs through the bell guard and divides the upper and lower areas. The blade divides the inside and outside areas.

In fencing there are **eight positions** for the weapon bearing arm. The names for these positions were introduced by the Italians. That is why the names are Italian.

We call them:
Prime (position No. 1), Seconde (No. 2), Tierce (No. 3), Quarte (No. 4), Quinte (No. 5), Sixte (No. 6), Septime (No. 7), and Octave (No. 8)

During the basic training for foil and epee, only three of the eight positions are taught: the Sixte, the Quarte, and the Octave. For saber it is the Tierce, the Quinte, and the Quarte. You can defeat any opponent with these three positions.

The Positions for Foil and Epee

Sixte.

If you are right-handed it is on the right, and if you are left-handed it is on the left. The arm is bent at a wide angle, the bell guard held between chest and waist.

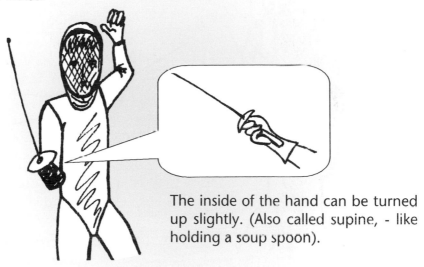

The inside of the hand can be turned up slightly. (Also called supine, - like holding a soup spoon).

When performing the Sixte position the following mistakes must be avoided:

The weapon is turned too far to the outside. This is not necessary for creating cover, but it does take up lots of time.

The tip of the blade points to the inside. The opponent's thrust can not be sufficiently averted this way.

Quarte

The **Quarte** is on the opposite of the Sixte.

Arm and bell guard are at the same level. The fist may be slightly turned down.

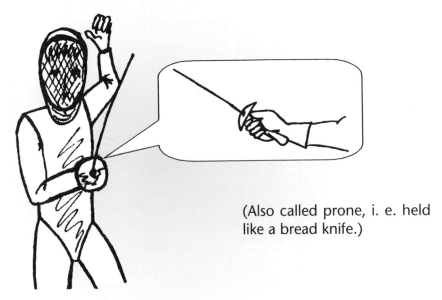

(Also called prone, i. e. held like a bread knife.)

When performing the Sixte position the following mistakes must be avoided:

The final position goes far beyond the threatened target area.

The tip of the blade points inward. The opponent's thrust can not be sufficiently averted this way.

Octave

The **Octave** is a lower position. It is located on the same side as the Sixte.

The bell guard is at the pelvic level and the tip of the blade points down and to the outside.

When performing the Octave position the following mistakes must be avoided:

The elbow is way too far to the outside.

Again the final position goes far beyond the threatened target area.

The Positions for Saber

With the saber you first learn these:

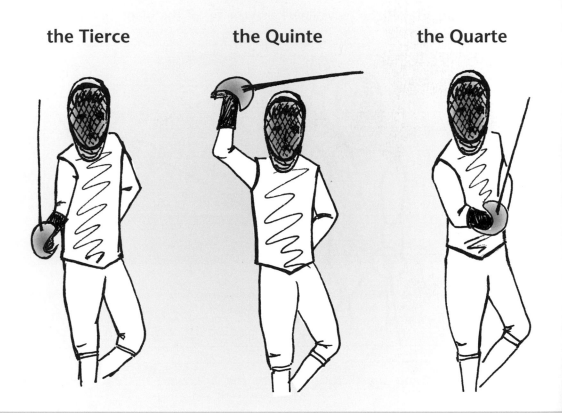

| the Tierce | the Quinte | the Quarte |

Typical mistakes must be avoided:

- *Don't exaggerate the positions.*
- *Move your weapon into position only as far as necessary to defend the threatened target area.*

Be sure to perform all positions in the most efficient way, and without reaching back. By reaching back first you lose precious time.

You will need to practice these positions diligently so for home you can perform them correctly with your eyes closed.

During partner exercises or lessons your target areas are continuously threatened. Make the right decision! In the beginning you have plenty of time to think about it, but gradually your decisions must come faster and faster.

Assume a fencing stance in front of the mirror and review the upper and lower openings, and the inside and outside openings. Then practice the described positions.

The Position Changes for Foil and Epee

Now you will learn how to move from one position to another. First you move from the basic stance into the position, and then back again.

From the basic stance into the Sixte position, and back:

- The weapon moves to the outside and upward at a slant.
- The blade and the arm form a straight line. Rotation occurs in the elbow.
- It's a little easier if you turn your wrist slightly to the outside (supine).

From the basic stance go into the Quarte position, and back again:

- You begin moving into the Quarte position with the tip of the blade, next with the wrist, and then the elbow follows.
- In the final position the hand is between chest and waist. The tip of the blade points slightly to the outside.

From the basic stance into the Octave position, and back again:

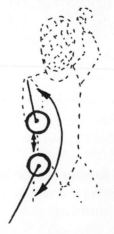

- You bring your blade into the Octave position with a semi-circular motion from the wrist.
- The blade points downward at a slant.

From the Sixte position into the Quarte position, and back again.

From the Sixte position into the Octave position, and back again.

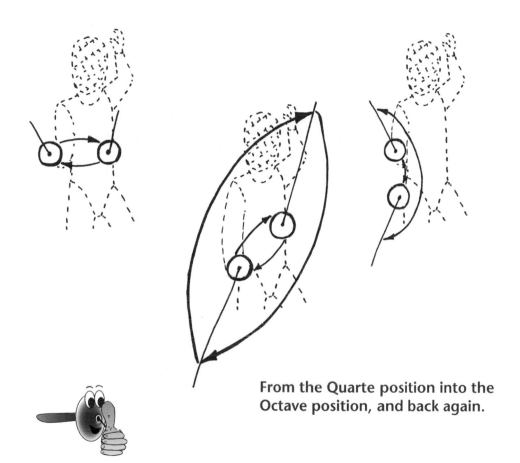

From the Quarte position into the Octave position, and back again.

Move the blade as efficiently as possible, without drawing back the arm! That takes up too much time.

You have to move the blade only as far as necessary to defend the threatened target area. So, don't "push" it too far to the outside.

Position Changes for the Saber

From the basic stance into the Quarte position, and back again.

From the basic stance into the Tierce position, and back again.

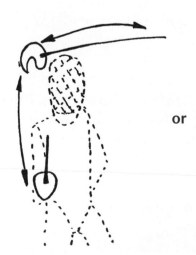

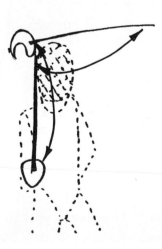

From the basic stance into the Quinte position.

or

It is important that the hand is slightly turned during the transitions. That way the blade always points a little to the outside.

Sweeping Moves

As the term "sweeping" indicates, you "sweep" the opponent's weapon from the target area if it is being (seriously) threatened by the opponent. The sweep is part of the parry technique. You will need these moves for your defense and for parry attacks. But we'll get back to that later.

Now you can put to use all the things we explained earlier:

- The respective movement corresponds with the change of **positions**.

- Your final stance corresponds with the **position** you take last, and it is called **engagement**.

The difference between this and the position changes is that the elimination move eliminates the opposing weapon from one's own target area.

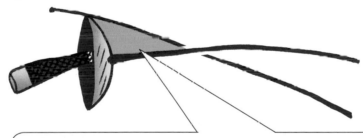

A triangle is formed between your bell guard, your forte (strongest part of the blade, and your foible (weakest part of the blade). Fencers call this triangle the control triangle or control point.

No matter which position you start in, you have to move your weapon in order to push your opponent's weapon out of your target area. It is best if your weapon is engaged at the end of the move.

Sweeps with the Foil and the Epee

Into the Sixte position

Into the Quarte position

Into the Octave position

You hold your opponent's blade with the beat.

In a bind it is always better to push the forte of your blade (the rear section) against the foible (front section) of your opponent's blade.

That makes you the stronger one and lets you control the opponent's weapon.

Sweeps with the Saber

If you are a saber fencer you should still read everything we wrote about the foil and the epee. Then look at the illustrations for the saber. It will help you understand them better.

Control triangles are not necessary against cuts.

.....9 Be Quick and Clever

Tactics Make Fencing Really Fun

Now you have the right equipment, you know the rules, and you've been working on technique. You can really get going now. But wait! That's not enough to win a bout. The most important part is missing.

There are a few "tricks" to defeating your opponent. You need to score without being touched yourself. To win you need to score more points and reach the winning score faster than your opponent does. That's the goal in fencing. And to do that you need tactics.

"Toucher sans l'être."
Scoring without being touched oneself.

Priority and Obligatory Defense

You have to attack the opponent to score a point. A correct **attack** begins with the arm extension and the threatening of the opponent's valid target area. If the arm is extended the step or lunge in the direction of the opponent will suddenly follow.

To keep the opponent from scoring you have to actively defend yourself. To defend yourself you can either retreat, or you push or strike the opponent's weapon aside. This is called **parry**. After a successful parry you can launch an attack yourself. This is called **riposte**.

A Bout Where One Wins and the Other Loses

A good fencer has a fighting spirit and good tactics. He or she must be able to execute the steps and the lunges quickly, and find the mark.

But more than anything a good fencer has brains. Tactics has a lot to do with thinking. In the end the one who just charges in won't win, but the smart one will. That's why a small fencer has a good chance against a taller one, because he can compensate for his lack of height with smarts.

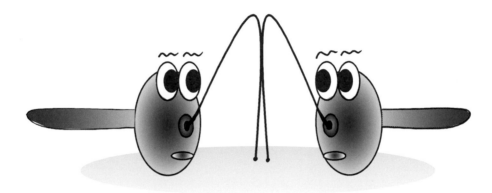

The Measure – Keeping the Right Distance

Let's go back to that cat again. When it tries to catch a mouse it sneaks up unnoticed until it can catch the mouse with one leap. Of course the fencer isn't trying to catch his opponent, but is trying to score a touch in a quick attack. To do that, he has to "sneak up" and wait until he has reached the right distance.

The distance between two fencers is called the measure. To make communication during training more efficient, the measure is divided into three different distances.

You can see this more clearly in the following illustrations.

Close measure
The fencers are standing so close together
that they can touch each other with their arms extended.

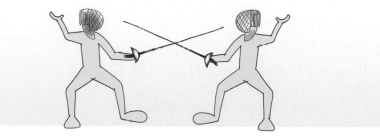

Middle measure
In addition to the arm extension
the fencer has to take a step or do a lunge to touch the opponent.

Far measure
Two leg movements are necessary to score a touch: step and lunge.

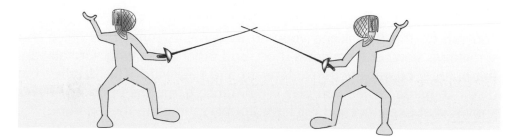

An opponent can quickly change the measure by taking a step backwards when being threatened. This is called "opening" the measure.

Practice forward and backward steps and lunges at varying speeds and rhythms: fast, slow, short or long, pausing, – then moving very quickly as if you were "exploding" .

The following is very important for tactics:

Learn to estimate the distance correctly

Remember that the measure you keep in a real bout depends on your technical skills as well as your opponent's speed. If you are able to execute a quick and long lunge, the measure can be longer. If you are very quick and good at defense you can shorten the measure.

Learn to hold the measure you want between you and your opponent

That way your opponent can't surprise you. A fencer who can estimate and keep a measure well is going to dominate his opponent. Good leg work is important here.

A fencer who moves like a snail won't be able to keep a measure.

Learn to bluff and outsmart your opponent when estimating and holding a measure

You can do this by making your leg movements sometimes quick and sometimes slow, or sometimes short, and other times long. Or you vary the number of steps you take forward and backward. This is called the **distance game**. When you play the distance game the opponent never knows what to expect and will have trouble estimating the measure.

The Moment – Timing Is Everything

Back to the cat that catches the mouse. Once it has found the right distance to the mouse it only has to find the right moment, and then jump.

In fencing the right timing for an attack or for defense is called the moment.

Surprise your opponent

An attack is most successful when the opponent is least expecting it. It is important that the opponent realizes too late when an attack is being launched, and therefore can't react fast enough. This requires good technique. From the fencing stance or the movement you can make an immediate lunge without any preliminary motion. So don't draw back first with your arms or legs.

Always be vigilant and don't let anyone surprise you

Always stay focused and watch your opponent carefully. Try to recognize by his movements what he is planning to do.

Distract and trick your opponent

When you imply a move during an engagement you will notice, that your opponent flinches as soon as he perceives your movement, and that he will anticipate an attack. Try to provoke a flinch and unsettle your opponent. You can distract and trick him this way. These sorts of tricks are allowed and fencers practice them.

Tactics are what we call this type of deliberate, clever, and also sly behavior which serves to surprise, distract, and trick the opponent. The opponent is being watched and his in- attention is being exploited. This is how you can create opportunities for scoring points.

93

Reactions

With these exercises you will learn to recognize the right moment and to react as fast as lightning. For a training partner, choose anyone who would have fun with it: friends, parents, grandparents, siblings, etc.

You are standing across from your partner, approx. a middle measure away, and are trying to slap your partner's hand.

If he manages to pull back his hand the moment you picked wasn't the right one. If you hit his hand you picked the right moment.

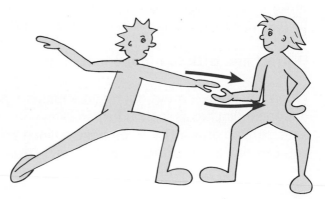

Good tacticians try to guess the strengths, weaknesses, and intentions of the opponent without showing their own, and to trick and outsmart the opponent. With tactics you learn to

94

use your technique and your form to defeat the opponent.

You partner places a coin or some other small object in his open palm. Place your hand underneath his and try to find the right moment to quickly grab the coin. Your partner can quickly pull his hand away. It's ok to reverse roles.

Your partner stands as shown in the illustration. His hands are about ten inches apart. Try to move your hands through the gap between your partner's hands. He should clap his hands together to catch yours.

Try to move your hand at varying speeds. You can trick and outsmart your partner like that.

Try the following and you will be amazed:

You start out really fast, and then stop just before you reach his hands. Of course he'll clap his hands together. When he opens them again, slowly move your hand through his.

95

Bridge boring waiting periods with games of skill

Surely you know of some situations where you just have to wait. At the gym, in the fencing hall for lessons to start, or at school.

How about some games of skill for those times? It'll be fun and the waiting time will pass much more quickly. You just have to be careful not to interfere with other people or with traffic.

Touching knees

Stand across from your partner and try to touch each others' knee with your hand. At the same time you need to avoid having you own knee touched. You can even choose teams.

Stepping on toes

Again you and your partner need to stand across from each other. Now try to step on each others toes. Watch out for your own toes!

Please remember:
It is all about skillfulness, not about hurting your partner!
Side by side

One partner tries to continuously stay at the right or left side of the other partner, who tries to shake him off by walking, running, or turning. (No spinning in circles!) See who can hang on the longest without being ditched.

Catch the glove

Your partner holds a glove or a similar object in his hand. You stand across from him. He will suddenly drop the object and you have to catch it before it touches the ground. Then you switch.

Write down some other games

that would be suitable and fun!

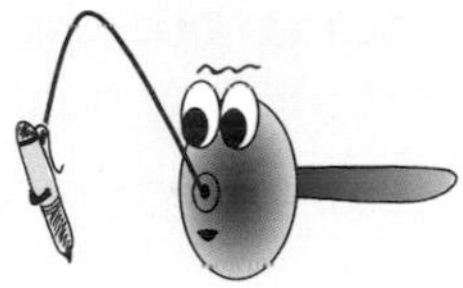

_____

_____

_____

_____

_____

_____

_____

_____

The Attack

Attack is the best form of defense!

You've probably heard this saying many times before. It also applies in fencing, because the attacker can determine the moment of the attack, and thereby holds the advantage.

The attacker chooses the moment to be at the correct measure. The attacker knows which type of attack he will use, and which technique he will apply. That is why he holds the advantage. From the rule book you learned that he who attacks first has priority.

How do you properly plan an attack?

1 You have been watching the opponent and you know that he doesn't want to attack first.

2 You perform the measure game and move the opponent to a distance that is advantageous to you. Don't follow the opponent, but try to attack him when he moves towards you.

3 When the right moment has come, attack without hesitation, determined and without preliminary movement. Remember, the attack begins with the extension of the arm.

This first type of attack you should launch is the direct attack with a direct thrust and a lunge. If you don't connect you need to immediately get up and retreat.

The Defense

In fencing there is a countermeasure to every measure.

Parry

When your opponent attacks, the first thing you need to do is defend yourself, so you can then launch your own attack. This type of defensive action is called a **parry**.

Displacement parry

You can retreat with a backward step or leap. This is called a **displacement parry**.

Blade parry

You can push the opponent's weapon aside with your own weapon. This is called a **blade parry**. (Also look in the book under "sweep".)

Keep practicing the transitions from one position to another. Look up the correct final positions for this in the book.

During a bind be careful not to draw the arm back first, or to make large, time consuming movements. However, your partner's blade must be firmly pushed away from your valid target area, and may not even touch you with an additional reach.

Making a successful defense

1 If you are always vigilant, your opponent won't be able to surprise you as easily. Learn to recognize from the slightest movement if your opponent is attacking. But don't give away your defense strategy too soon.

Have you ever watched a little bird? It is always vigilant so it can fly away as soon as a situation appears threatening. Always remember the vigilant bird when you are facing your opponent.

2 If you watch your opponent closely you may be able to tell where he will want to attack. Then you will know in advance which parry to use to fend off the attack, and you only have to concentrate on finding the right moment.

3 You can also bait your opponent into making an attack on a particular sector within the target area. This is also called an "invitation". For example, you can go into the Sixte position (Sixte invitation) and lure your opponent into an attack on the upper inside. Then you know that you can defend with a Quarte parry.

Sixte invitation   Octave invitation   Quarte invitation

Answering an Attack

After a successful parry you gain the priority. This means you need to move as quickly as possible to launch a counterattack – or to launch a **riposte**. It is said that a good engagement is like a debate. One person says something (attacks) and another person answers (defends). It constantly switches back and forth between attack, defense, and counter attack.

Or as we say in fencing talk: *Attack – Parry – Riposte*

Remember, the **riposte** is the attack that follows a parry, answering the opponent's attack.

How to make a successful riposte:

1 If you carry it out directly, quickly, and without delay, right after a successful parry.

2 If the opponent hasn't yet finished his attack. Then he can't parry your riposte.

It was nice to have a chance to talk with you again.

Now you can carry out a real bout with an attack, defense, and counter-attack. You can continue until the first fencer scores a valid point. But of course the object is to score a valid point with the first serious attack.

The Sweep Attack

You already know that you must first fend off a proper attack by your opponent before you can launch your own attack. And you also know that an attack begins with the arm extension and the threatening of the opponent's valid target area. But what happens if your opponent is constantly standing with "blade in line"? If you attack him with a direct thrust you'll also be touched, and don't gain priority. So you can only attack if you can push or knock your opponent's weapon aside. Then you can attack.

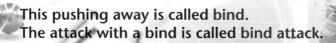

This pushing away is called bind.
The attack with a bind is called bind attack.

The blade action is called beat (also called battuta).
The attack with a beat is called a beat attack.

What's important in a sweep attack:

1 Don't draw back first, or your opponent will know your intentions.

2 Bind and beat are part of an attack, so don't pause in your forward movement.

3 Use these:
The **bind** with opponents who hold on tightly to their weapon and who tend to push back.
The **beat** with fencers who hold their weapon more lightly.

The Disengagement Attack

You should launch a disengagement attack if your opponent has you "caught" in a bind.

A semi-circle is made with the wrist. The arm is extended at the same time. The motion looks almost like the beginning of a spiral. The lunge begins when the arm is almost extended.

The disengagement attack is technically rather difficult. The disengaging of the opponent's bell guard happens quickly and without drawing back the arm. You can not touch the opponent's bell guard during disengagement. Otherwise the referee might think the opponent performed a parry.

If you are paying attention and you can perform the disengagement well, then try to already do it when your opponent wants to engage your blade or knock it aside.

103

The disengagement moves are prerequisites for a group of **combined attacks.** The most important ones are the **feint attacks.**

The Feint Attack

You use a feint to feign an attack. You pretend like you are seriously attacking your opponent and are trying to touch a particular spot.

As expected, your opponent will try to parry. You can then disengage this parry and score yourself.

1 The opponent shouldn't notice that you are only pretending to seriously attack. The feint attack should have the effect of a real attack. The measure and the moment the movement begins must be just right.

2 Feint attacks are only effective when you could also score with a direct attack. Otherwise the opponent isn't afraid and won't parry the way you expect him to.

3 Don't start your disengagement too soon, and always start at the speed at which your opponent parries.

Just a Few Rules to Help You Become a Tactically Smart Fencer

1 Every bout is a learning exercise. Even if you don't always win, be happy about every point you score, and don't get upset over points scored against you. But you should always know why you didn't make a touch or why someone touched you.

2 Apply the techniques you have practiced and mastered, but also try out some you would like to learn. Pay attention to measure and moment.

3 Observe what the opponent does well and not so well. Defeat him by exploiting his weaknesses. You should attack a good attacker first, and provoke a good defender to an attack.

4 Don't get upset about your opponent's fencing style. You have to find the right tools. Defeat your opponent with intelligence, and don't let the odd fencing style of your opponent unsettle you. Stay calm, especially with the "hotspurs".

5 When you have come to a decision, carry it out. Every hesitation is an opportunity for the opponent.

6 Try to force your will on your opponent. You determine the measure game, he has to follow you. Challenge him to certain attacks, and use the feint to force him into parries you want to disengage.

7 Be polite and fair at the fencing hall and on the fencing mat. Respect your opponent and the referee. Don't get angry about a decision, instead accept it and concentrate on your next action. The bout isn't over by a long shot if your opponent scores a point against you. You have every chance to win!

Conduct yourself like a fencer in everyday life, be confident and fair.

·········· 10 Keeping Things Straight

Almost everything in people's lives is regulated. It would be pretty chaotic if everyone could do whatever they please anytime, anywhere. Living together as a family usually involves following certain rules, and so does going to school. There are traffic rules for vehicles, and every game is played by rules.

It is no different in sports. Every sport has rules on how it should be practiced, how tournaments are run, and how scores are kept. The athlete is told when he has won and when he has lost, what is permissible according to the competition rules, and what is penalized.

In fencing the competition rules are also called **Reglement**. The entire fencing reglement is one big book. We will only write down the rules you need to know, to properly fence your first bouts. Remember that sport fencing as you are learning it now evolved from duels with sharp weapons. In order for this dangerous activity to develop into a non-dangerous sport, certain stipulations had to be instituted.

Some of these stipulations, also called **conventions**, have already been mentioned in the chapters about equipment and types of weapons. Think back to the different types of touches, the different target areas, and the priority.

On the following pages you will find out more about the rules you need to know for your first bouts.

The Fencing Strip (Piste)

In French the fencing strip is called piste. It must be level and have a skidproof covering. The strip is 60" to 80" wide. You can see the various marking lines and the specified measures in the illustration.

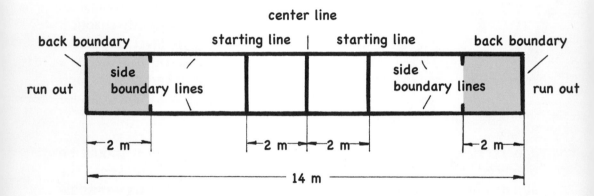

Tournaments are held on pistes made from conductive material. Usually the mesh is made from copper, but also aluminum or steel. Hits with the weapon to the ground are therefore not indicated.

Start of the bout

At the beginning of an engagement and after every point scored the fencers position themselves behind the **starting lines** on either side of the center line. After a time-out the action starts in the same spot where it was interrupted. The fencers face each other at such a distance that the tips of their blades don't touch when their arms are extended.

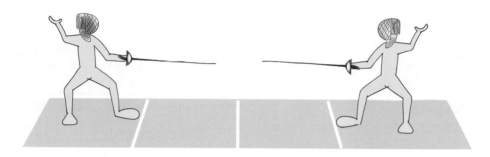

Here both fencers are positioned at the starting lines, waiting for the referee to say "Start!"

Crossing the boundaries

A penalty point is given for stepping over the back boundary line with both feet. Behind the end of the strip has to be a **run out** in case the fencer has too much momentum when dodging. The final 2m to the rear limit are clearly marked, preferably with a different color. This allows the fencers to easily gauge their position on the piste.

The fencers may not cross the **side boundary lines**. When a fencer crosses a **side boundary line** the referee interrupts the bout with a "Halt!" When a fencer has stepped off the fencing mat, he must reposition himself one meter behind his previous position. The other fencer faces him as he would after a time-out. If the fencer crosses the lateral boundary during an attack he must retreat 1m from the point where the attack was launched. If the "penalty meter" places him behind the rear limit he receives a penalty hit.

Some Information About the Competition

A fencing competition is called a **tournament**. The single combat in a tournament is called a **bout** or a **match**.

A practice bout that is fought according to the rules of the tournament is called **assaut**. At your qualifying tournament you have to demonstrate what you can do in such a practice bout against one or two other fencers.

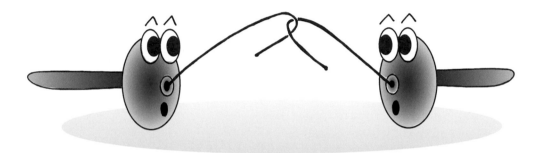

The tournament mode

Prior to a tournament the tournament mode is determined:

- Everyone fences against everyone in rounds, and the best two or three fencers move up to the next round.
- The **knockout** system is used in the direct elimination. Only the winner of each bout moves up. Sometimes there is a repechage during direct elimination.
- The **length of bout** (the maximum amount of time for a bout).
- The **winning point score** (how many points you need to score to win).

The length of bout and the winning point score are determined by the age group and the type of tournament. You will be given all of this information in time for the tournament.

At official tournaments of the German Fencing Association the student class fences with the small weapons for four points, with a pure length of bout maximum of four minutes. (During a pure length of bout the time-outs are not counted, instead the clock is stopped.)

Length of bout

The tournament management sets the rules for bout length and winning touch:

- In **rounds** – maximum of three minutes

- In **direct elimination** 10 hits in two 3-minute segments or 15 hits in three 3-minute segments. Each with a one minute break in-between.

- In **team competitions** three minutes for each individual bout.

The referee

The **referee** (or the representative) directs the bout. He gives the commands, observes the bout, and decides who gets the points. You could say that he is the boss, and it is his responsibility to make sure everything goes according to the rules.

This Is what a Bout in a Tournament Is Like

The call

The judges call the names of the fencers whose turn it is, and sometimes also the names of those whose turn it will be next. Whoever is called first stands on the right side of the referee.

If a right-hander fences against a left-hander, the left-hander always stands on the left side, even if he was called first.

These fencers are waiting to be called. What could they be thinking about?

The salute and the start of a bout

- First the fencers test their weapons and jackets for functionality.

- The fencers assume the basic position at their starting lines, and salute first the opponent and then the referee.

- When the command "on guard!" is given they assume a fencing stance. The referee than asks: *"Are you ready?"* or just *"Ready?"* If both fencers answer *"Yes"* the referee gives the command *"Start!"*, and the bout begins.

START!

In the fencing encyclopedia at the back of the book you can see the French terms used in international tournaments. The referee uses specific hand signals for the various commands.

When someone scores

The referee interrupts the bout with a "Halt!". The fencers must stop immediately and listen to the referee's remarks. He will describe the actions he observed, and whether one or the other fencer has scored a valid point.

As you already know, the bout will also be interrupted if someone crosses over the strip boundaries, or some other violations have occurred. If a valid point has been scored, the fencers return to their positions at the starting line. After other time-outs they pick up where they left off.

The end of the bout

The bout ends when one of the fencers has reached the winning point score, or when time is up. The current score applies after length of bout is reached.

The sport of fencing is no longer about life and death, but about fair competition!

That is why you should observe the following rules of conduct:

1 Fencing is a fair and "knightly" sport.

The most important principle is that of respecting the opponent and the practice partner.

You can only fence with another fencer. There would be no fencing without the athletic partner and opponent.

2 Always be honest.

Be honest with yourself. If you lose or something doesn't go the way you would like, don't blame others but try to find the fault within yourself.

Be honest with others. Don't cheat. Report a point scored when the referee didn't see it.

3 The referee is always right. You must follow his instructions implicitly.

If you think you scored and the referee doesn't agree, don't argue but ask him politely how he judged the touch. Fence correctly and properly, and every referee can understand your actions.

4 Fencing is a clean, "white" sport.

Always make sure you wear proper practice and tournament clothing.

Unsportsmanlike (unfair) conduct at a tournament is penalized by the referee.

115

There are three types of penalties:

The caution

- You enter the strip wearing improper clothing.
- You cover the target area with your free arm.
- If you cause a corps à corps (if you jostle the opponent).
- If you turn your back to the opponent to avoid being touched.
- If you leave the strip to avoid being touched.

When the referee issues a caution he shows the **"yellow card"**. The fencer then knows that he will receive a penalty point if he commits another violation.

The penalty point

A penalty point is given with a "red card". The fencers are immediately issued a **"red card"** if they:

- Exhibit unfair or un-sportsmanlike behavior, or are being deceitful.
- Fence too aggressively and injure the opponent intentionally.
- Repeatedly fail to follow the referee's instructions.
- A red card is issued for every offense following a yellow card.

Color in the penalty card held by the stick figure. You can color in the one on the following pages, too.

The disqualification

A **"black card"** may be issued for really bad offenses or for a repeat offense in the same bout. This means disqualification from the tournament. A "black card" is generally issued if:

- Someone tries to cheat; for example, by trying to significantly alter the equipment after the inspection.
- After begin of the tournament a fencer doesn't report after he has been called three times.
- A fencer deliberately strikes the opponent violently.
- A fencer refuses to deliver the salute at the start of a bout, or after the last point is scored
(it violates the spirit of good sportsmanship).

This is an abbreviated version of the rules for correct tournament equipment, some regulations, and the engagement procedures. Of course there are many more regulations, many exceptions and special rules, or new amendments. Your fencing instructor will explain those to you as required.

How will the referee rule?

A Word About the Referee

Hardly any fencer is satisfied with the referee's calls all of the time. That's probably also happened to you, or you have seen it happen. But in a tournament the referee is indispensable.

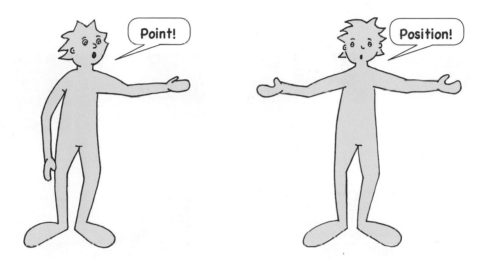

The tasks of a referee:

- He calls the fencers.
- He directs the bout.
- He enforces compliance with the safety rules.
- He inspects the fencers' equipment.
- He enforces order and discipline.
- He penalizes violations.
- He rules on points.

The referees have to be impartial. They can't favor a fencer or discriminate against one. An attack can happen very quickly. The fencers move forward and back, attack, parry, feint, and quick as lightning someone gets a point. The referee has to watch every move to see who the attacker was and who scored the point.

If you disagree with a decision, don't get upset, but quickly concentrate on the next attack. Being angry will only distract you, and complaining might even earn you a caution.

Just try it yourself. Watch a bout and think about how you would rule.

The Electronic Scoring Aid

When you are watching a fencing tournament with your parents or friends they probably ask you: "What is that ringing noise, and what do those flashing lights mean?" You answer: "Because fencing has such quick movements it is very difficult to follow. That is why the points are shown with an electronic signal."

Every time a fencer touches another fencer, one or two bulbs light up on his side of the electronic scoring aid.

This works like someone flipping on a light switch or pushing a bell button. The colored bulb (either red or green) comes on if the valid target area has been touched; the white bulb comes on if the invalid target area has been touched.

If both fencers', bulbs light up the referee has to decide whose touch was valid, and who gets the point. So he decides who gets priority.

The Round Format and the Scoreboard

In most individual tournaments elimination rounds are held prior to the disqualification round. Or the fencing rounds continue until the winner has been determined. The fencers are most often divided into rounds of six, but sometimes there may be five or seven fencers to a round. This depends on whether or not the number of tournament participants can be divided by six.

At the beginning of the tournament the tournament managers (the technical directors, or TD) determine how many fencers will move up, or continue to fence in each round. Usually there are three or four. The other fencers from that round are disqualified.

How such a round works in a student tournament.

In this round the fencers are Lisa, Peter, Anna, Tim, Julia, and Lucas. The fencers have already been entered on our **score sheet**.

No	Name	No	1	2	3	4	5	6	Vict.	Hits +	Hits -	Ind	Place
1	Lisa	1		V/4									
2	Peter	2	D/2										
3	Anna	3											
4	Tim	4					V/4						
5	Julia	5				D/3							
6	Lucas	6											

Every fencer fences against all the other fencers. The fencing order is predetermined in the tournament rules. You can see the fencing order listed on the scoreboard. The point score is also recorded here. We have already entered some of the results on the score sheet and on the scoreboard. Take another look at them so you can better understand the example.

And now an example:

It begins with the first bout of Number **1** (Lisa) against Number **2** (Peter). In the course of the engagement a slash is made on the score sheet for every touch a fencer scores. This makes it easy to keep track of the results. As you can see from the score sheet, Lisa had **four** touches in the first bout, and Peter had only **two**, which means Lisa won **4:2**. You can also see the order in which the touches occurred. The slashes are staggered. First Lisa scored two touches and then Peter and Lisa scored by turns.

This result is recorded on the score sheet. In row No. 1 (it says Lisa), column No. 2 (that's Peter's column) A "**V**" is entered for "Victoire", the French word for victory. The number of points is entered after the slash (so **V/4**). For Peter a "**D**" (that's short for the French word "Défaite", meaning defeat) and the number of points scored (**D/2**) is entered in row 2, column 1 (that's Lisa's column).

The second bout is also entered on our sample score sheet. According to the set fencing order No. 4 will fence against No. 5, that's Tim against Julia. This bout ends with a 4:3 win for Tim.

1	// // V/4	5	/// / V/4	2	///	1	//	5	/
2	// D/2	6	// / D/3	5	// //	6	/ / //	1	// //
4	//// V/4	3	// / D/3	1	/	4	/// /	3	/
5	/// D/3	1	/ /// V/4	4	/// /	2	//	4	// //
2	// // V/4	6	/ D/1	5	/	3	/ ///	6	/ / //
3	// / D/3	4	// // V/4	3	////	6	/	2	//

The referee forgot to enter the results of the next four bouts on the score sheet. He simply entered slashes for the remaining four bouts.

Now you are the assistant referee. Complete the score sheet and properly enter the results on the scoreboard. Maybe you can already fill in the empty boxes on the sample form.

Puzzle

1. Traditional hilt with finger rings and crossbar
2. A block of the attack
3. A movement forward
4. When the blades are in contact with each other
5. One of the three types of weapons
6. Parry #3

7. Solution: moving the target to avoid an attack; dodge

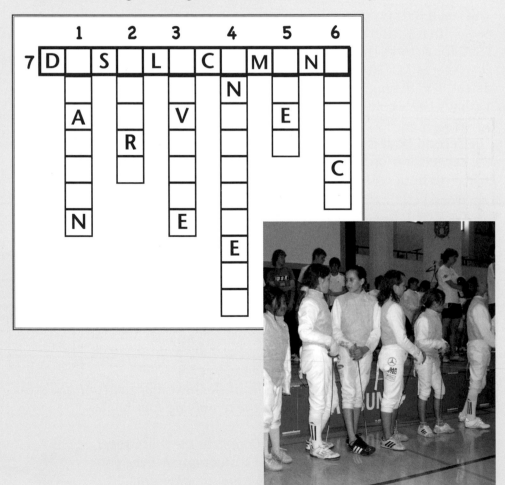

	1	2	3	4	5	6
7	D	S	L	C	M	N
				N		
	A		V		E	
		R				
						C
	N		E			
				E		

For Practice

You can copy this blank score sheet and score board and use them for practice in training bouts.

At this point you don't have to be able to calculate and fill in the information on the score sheet. It is a little too complicated for basic education students. But if you are interested, ask your fencing instructor or another older fencer to explain it to you.

Date: _____

No	Name	No	1	2	3	4	5	6	Vict.	Hits +	Hits -	Ind	Place
1		1											
2		2											
3		3											
4		4											
5		5											
6		6											

1		5		2		1		5	
2		6		5		6		1	
4		3		1		4		3	
5		1		4		2		4	
2		6		5		3		6	
3		4		3		6		2	

Winner: _____

125

...................11 Fit and Healthy

Most people who are active in a sport want to have fun and make achievements. But another importantgoal for athletes is being healthy and keeping your body fit.

Eating Right

Someone who is active in a sport uses more energy than a couch potato. That's why food always tastes best after practice, because you're hungry! All kids love to eat candy bars, chips, fries, and pizza. That's not exactly the right food for an athlete, particularly if you eat these foods often, and in large quantities. These types of food contain way too much fat.

Better nutrition would include pasta, bread, and rice dishes, as well as smaller portions of meat, fish, and poultry. Add to that lowfat milk and dairy products like yoghurt and cheese. You get your essential vitamins from fruit, vegetables, and salad. As you can see, there are lots of healthy foods that taste good, too.

 *Try to have a varied and moderate diet.*

127

If You Sweat a Lot, You Have to Drink a Lot

Oh no, my belly is so full! And I was only thirsty!

When you sweat you lose a lot of water, which you need to replenish by drinking sufficiently. You can still drink sweetened beverages just before your practice or before a tournament. But during your practice or tournament breaks you should stick with water, water mixed with juice, or tea (maybe sweetened with a little honey).

When you are thirsty and drink something, make sure you don't drink too fast. It is better to take frequent small sips.

Beverages should not be ice cold. It is bad for your stomach and takes too much energy away from your body.

Hello, Doc!

"Hello, Doc", is what you will say cheerfully to your doctor, because as an athlete you feel terrific most of the time. But even if you are not sick you should see your doctor at least once a year for a checkup.

Tell him that you are learning to fence and explain what you do during your practice sessions. He will examine you and most likely determine that you can fence without any health concerns.

Have your vaccination record updated, and get some nutrition tips!

Warm-up

Surely your coach includes a warmup at the beginning of a practice session. It is important to warm and loosen up your muscles with different exercises. This helps to protect you from injury. To warm up you can jog and skip, bend and stretch, and then shake out your limbs.

Muscle soreness is not an illness! When your muscles must perform unfamiliar movements or work hard it can result in sore muscles. If something hurts, tell your coach and your parents. That is very important!

Exercises for home

Here you will find some exercises to do in the morning, or as a warm-up.

To warm up, you can jog or do some easy jumping exercices.

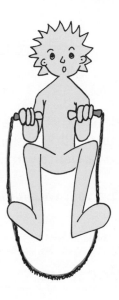

Strech really tall and stand on your toes at the same time, like you are trying to pick apples.

Now collapse suddenly and makeyourself really small.

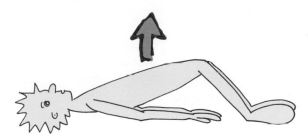

Lie flat on your back and push your pelvis upward.

Rotate your hips from side to side.

Bend your torso to the right and to the left.

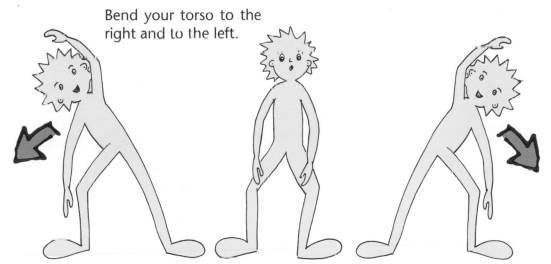

Do you sometimes have problems getting going in the morning? These exercicises are also well suited as morning calisthenics.

More exercises

Here you can write down more exercises and make drawings of them.

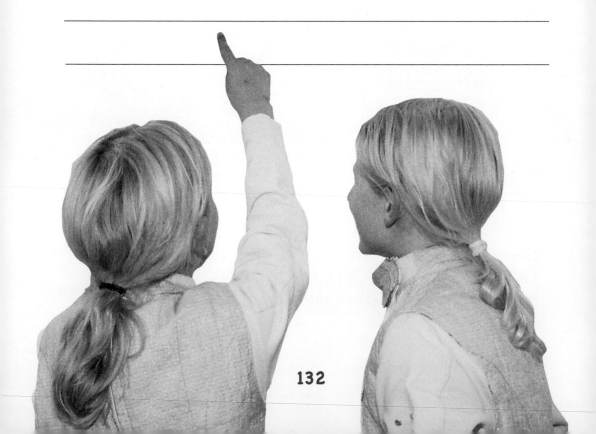

A Successful Day Begins with a Good Start in the Morning

When the alarm goes off or your parents call, don't turn back over, but get out of bed.

Think about what you're going to do that day, and what you look forward to. That will help you get up quicker.

 Morning gymnastics will help you to wake up and get going. Just a few minutes are enough to get your blood moving. (You can find some suitable exercises on the following page.)

After the exercises it is time to get cleaned up. Finish up with a cold shower. It strengthens the body's defenses and helps protect you from getting colds.

Take your time with breakfast, and sit down while you eat. Eat something that is healthy and tastes good. Milk, milk products, or cereal, whole grain bread and some fruit. Don't forget to brush your teeth.

Leave for school on time so you don't have to rush. You will avoid stress first thing in the morning, focus better on your classes, and still have energy for your fencing lesson after school.

This athlete is really hungry after practice. He would like to just eat and drink everything at once. What would you recommend? Cross out anything that in your opinion is not very healthy!

1

Which food should you eat more frequently during the day, and when you need a snack? Cross out every L, Y, M, A, X, E, K and D.

F	D	K	A	R	E	X	Y	M	L	A
M	E	L	M	A	U	D	I	K	D	Y
Y	A	D	D	L	K	Y	M	A	M	T

2

...............12 Ready For a Tournament

Fencing is a clean and fair sport for which you need special equipment, and it has set rules and regulations.

You would probably be very surprised if your opponent would appear at a foil tournament in sweat-pants and without a mask, wildly swinging an old saber, and pretending he knows how to fence. To keep things like that from happening, only certified participants are permitted to fence at a tournament. In other words, only those people who can prove that they know how to fence.

Some fencing associations or clubs have their young fencers take a fencing exam. Only those fencers who can prove that they can fence and know the rules are permitted to fence in tournaments.

But don't worry, if you've been practicing and have paid attention to your instructor, you'll be ready for a tournament. Besides, you have your "magic bullet", the fencing book for children. And your friend "Foily" has been telling you how to perform the correct sequence of fencing moves, and which rules you need to obey.

On the next few pages you can test your fencing knowledge, and what you have learned so far. Answer all the questions, filled out everything, and show the movements.

You can take the test with your training group or some of your friends. Don't forget safety!

In the **aptitude exam** you have to show what you know about fencing, and that you can properly execute the most important techniques.

In the **practical exam** you have to show that you can apply your knowledge and skills in actual bouts.

And if you're unsure, take another look in the book!

Some Questions About Fencing and the Protective Equipment

Question 1: What is the name of your fencing club and your national fencing association?

_____

_____

Question 2: What are the types of weapons used in the sport of fencing? Which weapons do men and boys use, and which weapons do women and girls use?

_____

_____

Question 3: Explain to your friend what type of sport fencing is, what's important about it, and why you like to fence.

_____

_____

Question 4: Is fencing dangerous? What do you have to do to protect yourself? Name all the equipment required for a fencing bout.

_____

_____

Some Questions About Tournament Rules

Question 5: Name the most important stipulations (conventions) for each of the three disciplines of fencing.

foil

_____

_____

epee

_____

_____

saber

_____

_____

Fill in the valid target areas on the three figures.

foil   epee   saber

Question 6: What do you call the surface on which a fencing bout takes place? Explain to your parents the size of the area, its boundary lines and what they mean. What happens if you cross over those lines? Are there differences between those lines?

_____

_____

Question 7: What must you do when the referee calls your name to fence?

_____

_____

Question 8: What age group are you fencing in? What other age groups are there for children and adolescents?

_____

_____

Question 9: What is a "caution" and how is it issued? How is a penalty point indicated and how do you get one? What does the "black card" mean?

_____

_____

Question 10: What is the referee's task?

_____

_____

Learning Fencing

Exercise:
Explain the rows and columns on the score sheet and the score board. What is recorded here and how is the winner determined?

No	Name	No	1	2	3	4	5	6	Vict.	Hits +	Hits -	Ind	Place
1		1	■										
2		2		■									
3		3			■								
4		4				■							
5		5					■						
6		6						■					

1		5		2		1		5	
2		6		5		6		1	
4		3		1		4		3	
5		1		4		2		4	
2		6		5		3		6	
3		4		3		6		2	

_____

_____

_____

_____

_____

_____

Exercises for Technique and Tactics

After you have really practiced the techniques in exercises 1 and 2, ask your fencing instructor if he is satisfied. If he is satisfied, then ask him to sign off on the individual techniques in your book with his **signature**.

Exercise 1:

Correctly perform the following **leg technique elements** and explain what is most important about each one.

1. Basic stance and fencing stance
2. Forward step and backward step
3. Lunge and recovery from lunge
4. Forward steps and backward steps
    at different speeds (slow or fast), and
    different lengths (short and long steps)

Exercise 2:

Correctly perform the following technical **blade technique elements**, and explain what is most important about each one.

1. Fencer's salute
2. Blade in line
3. Three blade positions with the weapon
4. Changes in blade position

Exercise 3:

With a partner correctly **perform fencing action**, and explain what is most important.

1. Determine the measure by making forward and backward steps. Launch a direct attack at the moment when your partner switches from the fencing stance to a position.

2. Be careful to keep the correct measure. Which measure is used in a lunge attack?

3. Use the parries you know to fend off a direct attack. What do you need to remember?

4. Answer your partner's attempt to bind your blade in line from various directions, or to push it away, with a disengagement attack.

5. What is a feint attack? With a partner demonstrate a feint attack in an exercise chosen by you. hat do you have to pay close attention to?

Exercise 4:

In practice bouts with a training partner demonstrate that you are able to properly apply technique and tactics in a tournament setting.

.... 13 Little Fencing Encyclopedia

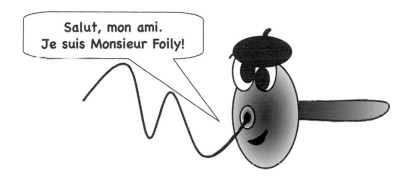

Salut, mon ami. Je suis Monsieur Foily!

As you know, the official language for fencing is French.

Here you can find some French terms and expressions used by the referee in international tournaments

You already use some French terms in your practice sessions. You probably also noticed some French terms while reading this book. These words are pronounced a little differently than what we are used to in English. Ask your fencing instructor to help you with the proper pronunciation.

Reglement	tournament rules
Piste	(fencing) strip
Tableau	form on which the names, victories, defeats, and points are recorded
Victoire	victory

Défaite	defeat
Assaut	practice bout
Riposte	return attack
En piste les numéros trois et six, s'il vous plaît...	Number three and six on the piste (strip), please...
En garde!	On guard!
Allez!	Begin!
Halte!	Halt!
L'attaque part de gauche/ à droit touché.	attack from left/right touched
L'attaque à droit passe.	attack from right missed
L'attaque est non valable.	invalid attack
Assaut terminé!	Bout over!

Here you can write down some more words and expressions you want to remember.

_____

_____

_____

_____

.... 14 Solutions and Answers

This is where I give you the solutions to the puzzles and the answers to my questions.

Page 38

Nine pieces of fencing equipment.

M	H	K	A	T	R	M	G	S	G	V	O	U	I	L
H	F	O	P	A	I	T	T	B	K	O	L	S	F	X
I	E	C	H	P	R	O	W	O	K	S	A	B	E	R
A	N	G	X	U	C	L	I	D	C	A	F	E	N	I
S	C	L	M	K	M	D	A	Y	C	L	O	N	C	A
R	I	P	I	H	P	Z	E	C	T	O	I	T	I	K
L	N	N	M	A	S	K	T	A	S	K	L	L	N	O
E	G	C	E	S	P	I	S	B	M	U	D	U	G	L
S	J	L	E	U	J	A	N	L	A	V	L	O	S	T
S	A	U	A	W	E	B	P	E	V	B	O	W	H	Y
R	C	A	R	G	Z	P	K	N	A	F	R	O	O	R
P	K	N	B	D	D	Z	E	P	U	M	J	Y	E	K
L	E	O	K	G	L	O	V	E	C	P	Z	U	S	A
U	T	N	A	E	G	A	S	L	V	E	F	E	L	M
K	L	O	G	W	E	G	B	S	L	N	A	H	U	U
C	E	F	R	D	P	T	M	B	D	A	I	R	R	I

The most important differences between the two fencers:

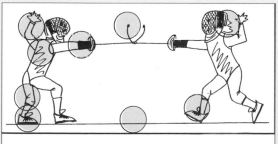

Page 46

1 – A

2 – C

3 – B

Page 63

Fencing stance, corrections on the five figures.

No. 1 Bends over; the torso is not upright.
No. 2 Leans too far back, as if afraid; the rear leg "hangs" back.
No. 3 Weapon bearing arm is too close to the body; the rear leg is not bent.
No. 4 Stands too upright.
No. 5 Arms are bent too much; feet too close together; the rear foot outward and not at a right angle; fencer is not looking forward.

Page 68

No. 1 is not extending his weapon bearing arm at the beginning of the attack.
No. 2 is "climbing" into the lunge as if he were jumping onto a chair.
No. 3 has placed the foot of his lunging leg too far forward, the pivot leg is not extended, and he is "dancing" on his toes.
No. 3 does not place the foot of the pivot leg forward enough, and therefore has to reset that foot so he can reach the opponent.
No. 4 has his torso bent over so far, that it looks like he will fall over.

Page 70

Recovery from the lunge, corrections on the two figures.

No. 1   This fencer is "climbing" out of the lunge and has trouble retur-
        ning to the fencing stance quickly.
No. 2   The torso always remains upright during recovery from a lunge.
        The legs do all the work. This fencer is leaning back and looks
        like he has no strengthin his legs.

Page 72

Setting up the thrust, corrections on the three figures.

No. 1   The thrust must be a "beeline" for the target area. Don't pull your
        arm in and try to "strike out" like a boxer!
No. 2   The move is performed only with the arm, and not by leaning
        forward with your torso.
No. 3   This fencer looks as though he is afraid of is opponent. Don't lean
        back! You won't be able to reach your opponent that way.

Page 114

That can't happen! The white bulbs indicate invalid touches which don't
apply in epee fencing. As you know, in epee fencing the entire body is a
target area.

Page 118

No. 1   He fences too aggressively and injure the opponent intentionally.
No. 2   He is being deceitful.
No. 3   He is trying to significantly alter the equipment.

Page 124

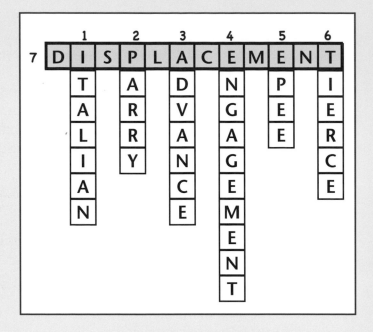

Page 134

F	D	K	A	R	E	X	Y	M	L	A
M	E	L	M	A	U	D	I	K	D	Y
Y	A	D	D	L	K	Y	M	A	M	T

.... 15 Let's Talk

Dear Fencing Parents:

You should be pleased! Your child has made a great choice with the sport of fencing.

Fencing distinguishes itself by its variety of movements, it demands a high degree of dexterity, and promotes concentration, critical thinking, and quick decision making.

You child is part of a group of children training together and also fencing bouts against each other. The young fencer is integrated into the group and at the same time challenged by it. He learns to assert himself, and to deal with success and failure in minor tournaments. All of these skills are cultivated by fencing, and your child will be able to apply them in other areas of life, such as school, or later on in his professional life.

Your child is learning a sport not everyone can do. The proverbial "chivalry" means fairness and respect for others.

Please support your child in learning and practicing fencing, and help develop and maintain his or her enthusiasm for practice, learning, and athletic competition.

With the help of "Learning Fencing" your child will understand the sport of fencing more easily and learn more quickly. This book is written for children age nine to eleven.

Ideally the education should start with

The Basics of Fencing.

The basic fencing education is the same for all "newcomers", regardless of whether your child wants to fence on a competitive level if it turns out that he or she is particularly talented, or not.

> "Mom, can I start fencing now? I'm already two years old, and I have my own saber!"

During this first part of fencing education the goal is to create a multilateral foundation of motor qualification, and to experience various types of movement.

The children should enjoy practicing, and should learn the basics of fencing through a variety of methods. The percentage of actual fencing during this basic education is approx. 40%. So it is for a purpose if your child also does gymnastics and plays soccer during fencing class, or swims in summer and skis in winter.

The fencing exam marks the end of the basic education. This is when your child earns the fencing certificate, and with it the right to participate in official fencing tournaments.

The basic education is followed by the

Principles of Fencing Training.

During this next step begins the systematic increase in performance as your child becomes faster and stronger, perfects his technique and tactics, and participates regularly in tournaments.

Be Helpful, but with Prudence.

Don't expect more of your child than he or she can do, or is willing to do at the moment. Don't make comparisons with other children of the same age. Physical development still varies a lot at this age. Take your cue from your child and praise his or her progress. Your child will thank you.

It is our intention to facilitate long-term, systematic, and age appropriate training based on these recommendations. Excessive ambition during the basic fencing education can be damaging.

Dear Fencing Instructor:

Surely you'll agree that it is a great feeling to see these little guys stand before you, their faces full of curiosity and their eyes wide with anticipation. The responsibility for their fencing education now lies in your hands.

But each of these children is different from the other. There are the hard-working ones and the not-so-hardworking ones, the talented ones and the not-so-talented ones, the precocious ones and the late bloomers.

Each child is a little individual with his or her individual background and developmental history, with hopes and desires, with its existential orientation and needs. All of them are worthy of our attention, our care, and our love.

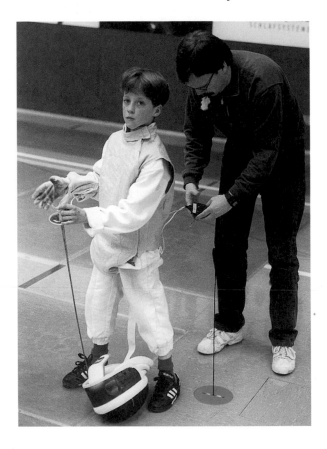

The more a fencing instructor is able to relate to his fencing children, empathizes with them, is accessible to them, and inspires them, the more effective he will be.

He has to encourage them and listen to them, sympathize with them, praise and comfort them, in short, he needs to love children. He also has to be able to put the brakes on a hot head or issue a reprimand. But he always does so respectfully.

What a Children's Fencing Instructor Must Have

The Value of this Little Book

will depend entirely on how it is integrated into the fencing education. It is written specifically for children who are completing the basic fencing education.

But it is also recommended for parents who want to know what to expect if their child is interested in fencing, and wants to learn the sport.

This material also helps provide a basis for communication for faster learning progress with children who are already fencing. Most of the tutorials and fencing books don't focus enough on the actual actors, the fencers themselves, even though they represent the most important part of the teaching and learning process. A fencer, even if he is young and a total beginner, is always subject to his own progression, and never an object to be influenced by us.

Offer them plenty of support and opportunity for their own growth. Promote and make use of your fencing children's independence. Take the road from "instructing" to "inspiring".

The book focuses on the needs of the children, and is meant to encourage them to also engage in fencing related activities outside of the fencing hall. The book's illustrations and descriptions of the most important techniques provide the child with a fairly complete foundation for practicing. He or she will be able to better follow your instructions and demonstrations.

The fencing children can reread what they have learned, and get suggestions for practicing at home, with other children or in front of the mirror. This develops the ability to act independently and speeds up the learning process. An environment is created in which the children are encouraged to think about their own practicing and learning, their movements and actions, and lastly to examine and to evaluate their performance. They become a partner to the fencing instructor. This is the ideal objective for the beginning instruction. We would like the children to look forward to coming to fencing class, and to go home with a sense of achievement. And of course it would make the practice sessions fun for the fencing instructor, too.

Finally we would like to make some recommendations regarding the application of this book in your work as a fencing instructor:

- Explain to the children that this book is their personal guide during their fencing education. Give them a copy of your club logo and take a group photo they can paste in their copy of the book. This will help the bonding process with you, and promote commitment to the club, and the sport.

- Help the children to properly work with the book. In the beginning read some of the chapters together, and talk about how the photos and illustrations should be looked at and interpreted. This creates important orientation guides for understanding and promotes independent practice.

- Ask the children to complete the exercises. Demonstrate and explain the new techniques or actions, and practice them in fencing class. Then tell the children to review the technique (position and movement) at home. Anyone who wants to can demonstrate and explain the new material to the other children at the next practice session.

- If you are planning on teaching something that requires some preliminary work, ask the children to prepare themselves for the lesson. For example, you might say: "Next lesson we will learn to do sweeping movements. You will need to really know the positions. Take another look at the book, then practice at home and check each others form, or use a mirror. Kelly and Peter will demonstrate them for us, and we will all determine if they are doing it right or if we have to correct them."

- If a child has to miss a lesson tell him what you will be working on that day, and recommend that he read about that material in the book. That way the children won't all have to repeat the material, and you can avoid monotony.

- We tried to write the book in language that is child and age appropriate, and to include graphic explanations whenever possible. By using the same or similar phrasing you can ensure a common basis for communication within the practice group, and cut down on explanations and corrections during practice sessions. This will free up more time for actual practicing.

- In the book we used the terms fencing "instructor" and "practice session", because the basic fencing education focuses on the very basics of fencing, and does not yet include "training" in the true sense of the word.

We welcome any critical commentaries or additions.

We wish you and your little protégées lots of fun and enjoyment, and many fencing successes.

.... Photo & Illustration Credits

Cover graphics:	Thinkstock
Cover design & typesetting:	Sannah Inderelst
Illustrations:	Katrin Barth
Photos:	Melanie Ebert-Exner, Steffen-Michael Eigner, Friethjof Fischborn, Foto-Zentrum Leipzig, Hilde Joppich, Xavier Marest, Ingo Stafehl, FC Tauberbischofsheim, Olaf Wolf, Adobe Stock

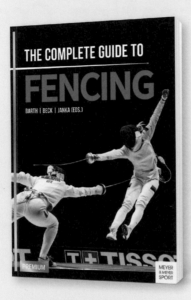

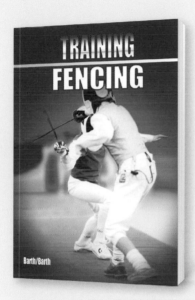

Barth/Barth

TRAINING FENCING

2nd edition
152 p., in color
21 photos + 249 illus.
Paperback, 5 3/4" x 8 1/4"
ISBN: 9781841260969

$ 14.95 US/£ 9.95 UK/€ 14.95

Building on the book *Learning Fencing*, this book explains how to train for the techniques and tactics in the sport of fencing and shows why fencers must improve their endurance, strength, and speed. Young fencers learn to go beyond practice bouts and enrich their training with exercises that may seem to have nothing at all to do with fencing. They discover how important it is to warm up before training and competitions and learn why an athlete gets stiff muscles. The book also includes suggestions about what young athletes can do on their own to improve their skills and to monitor and evaluate their progress. With the help of this book, young fencers learn to manage their own development and to take responsibility for their own behavior.

MEYER & MEYER Sport   Phone   +49 241 - 9 58 10 - 13
Von-Coels-Str. 390   Fax   +49 241 - 9 58 10 - 10
52080 Aachen   E-mail   sales@m-m-sports.com
                                 Website   www.m-m-sports.com

All books available as e-books.

MEYER
& MEYER
SPORT